DUMB DICKIE

A MEMOIR OF LEARNING, GROWTH, HOPE, AND BLUNDERS

RICHARD E. KLEIN

DUMB
DICKIE
PRESS.

Published by Dumb Dickie Press

ISBN-13: 978-1-0894-1018-8
ISBN-10: 1-0894-1018-2

Cover design by Ellen Meyer and Vicki Lesage

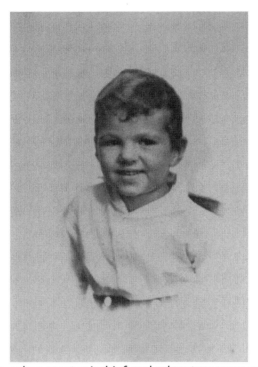

Dickie Klein, when most mischief and adventure were yet to come.
Photograph was taken circa 1942.

DEDICATION

Lieutenant, Junior Grade Frank John Malinski

I wish to dedicate this book to the memory of Frank J. Malinski, Jr. (1939-1963). Frank Malinski was a close friend and kind individual. I first met Frank when he joined Troop 202, Boy Scouts of America, when he was about age 12. He and his mother had moved from Eastern Pennsylvania to Stratford, Connecticut. Frank graduated from College of the Holy Cross, Hartford, in 1961, where he had been enrolled in the U.S. Navy R.O.T.C. program. Upon graduation, Frank was commissioned as an officer in the U.S. Navy. Frank was aboard the nuclear-powered submarine USS Thresher. The USS Thresher with its complement of 129 men and officers sank on April 10, 1963. The USS Thresher was undergoing deep-dive trials after having been refitted at Portsmouth Naval Shipyard, Portsmouth, New Hampshire. Frank was one of four officers on board. To this day, the U.S. Navy makes few statements as to the exact cause of the loss. The USS Thresher now lies in about 8,400 feet of water in the Atlantic east of Cape Cod. It came to rest precariously on the edge of the Continental Shelf. Because of its precarious position, no effort has been made to recover the USS Thresher.

TABLE OF CONTENTS

INTRODUCTION

It is important to be able to laugh at yourself. Dumbness surrounds us and is abundant. There is no scarcity of dumbness. I consider myself to have been smart enough to recognize and admit that I was dumb. You can never learn from your mistakes until you can recognize them. A consistent theme throughout this book is that I recount mistake upon mistake, but then use those mistakes and the lessons learned to mature in wisdom.

I recount some of the dumber things I have done in my lifetime. Note that I said "some of" and certainly not all, and certainly not the very dumbest. My worst transgressions remain matters that God will deal with. My purposes in writing are to have a little fun and to impart a little wisdom from my personal history. As such, this book is in part an autobiography.

The events described in *Dumb Dickie* actually happened. This compilation spans eight decades. I have told many stories based on memory. While memory is good to have, it can be fickle. If any errors or misrepresentations arise, they are not intentional. I have given names, dates, and places, all to the best of my ability and memory. No effort has been made to mask or hide identities. All persons described, whether pure as the driven snow or dark and evil, are named. I have no wish to protect the guilty.

CHILDHOOD MEMORIES

Dumb Dickie Embarks on a Path of Foolishness at a Young Age
(1939-1957)

The Early Years

I STARTED OFF early in life doing dumb things and having a mind of my own. My mother, Ellen Moller Kristensen Klein (1914-2002), married at age 19. It was a dark time—during the Great Economic Depression. The depression was at near bottom when she eloped on December 11, 1933.

My brother Donald Albert was born September 11, 1935. Frederick Walter followed on February 6, 1938. Although I was conceived some cold night in May of 1938, my mother had no inkling or clue that I was conceived aboard. She only realized my presence on Labor Day weekend, 1938. She went to put on her bathing suit, but somehow she couldn't get it on. My mother later explained to me that I was a perfect child, at least during her pregnancy. She never experienced morning sickness or nausea. Because I was so well behaved in her womb, she was certain she was carrying a girl. But there was no question about one thing. I was not a planned child. Moreover, in the days of coming out of the depression, I wasn't wanted either.

In 2002, following my mother's passing, I was surprised to find the receipt for her hospital stay when I was born. That one aged piece of paper speaks volumes about what a dollar was worth then compared to today.

The bill for an entire week in the hospital for my mother and me totaled less than twenty-five dollars. The $24.25 bill also included the delivery room charge. I note with some interest that my father wasn't able to pay the bill in full. He was short by $6.50.

In her golden years before her passing, I spoke with Mother about my birth. She and I had become comfortable with virtually any and all topics. Mother never volunteered to tell me things, but whenever I asked a specific question, she answered. Back in the era of her delivering me, the standard medical practice was for the mother to remain in bed for days following the birth. She could not get up and walk about. She had to use a bed pan as opposed to a toilet. A second practice was to give the expectant mother a sedative to render her unconscious during labor and delivery. Mother told me she fought this because she wanted to be conscious.

Nine months earlier, while I was being conceived, I did a dumb thing—I was male. After having two boys, my mother was convinced I was going to be a girl. The name was picked: Carolyn. When I arrived and announced myself as a boy on February 11, 1939, my mother was stymied. She didn't have a name in mind.

As I have recently engaged in family history, I happened to find a letter written by my mother concerning names. She wrote some four years after my birth, on May 4, 1943, about her philosophy of naming things. My mother was a particular lady. In her mind, as her letter attested, a name (or specifically, a boat's name) had to possess certain attributes. It needed to be light, frivolous, and odd. My guess was that because she was so particular about coming up with a name for me, she got writer's block. According to what she told me when I asked, she ended up looking in a book of names provided for new mothers. She selected Richard Earl Klein. Looking back, I note that my name was quite Anglicized. My two older brothers were given names with a greater Germanic tone, at least for 1930s America.

As a kid growing up, I was dumb. It certainly didn't help that I was surrounded by dumb people. This included parents, brothers, teachers, and more teachers. Here are just some of the dumb things I was told and expected to swallow whole:

- You must chew your milk.
- Polio comes from houseflies.
- If you don't eat the vegetables on your plate, some child in China will starve.
- The American dollar is sound; it is backed by gold.
- If you don't wait twenty minutes after eating to swim, you will get a cramp and drown.
- All energy comes from the sun.
- You can't divide by zero.
- A bicycle doesn't fall over because the spinning of the wheels gyroscopically stabilizes the bike.
- The whole car gets there at the same time.
- A little cod-liver oil will do the trick.
- The temperature of the ocean is a constant.
- You can't get into college unless you take two foreign languages in high school.
- If only we had base-twelve, division by three would be

possible.

- Payable in silver to the bearer on demand.
- A wind-up (model) train is just as good as an electric train.
- Sunoco gasoline is no good; I can tell as my car doesn't like it.
- Inside air is bad, you must sleep at night with all the bedroom windows open.
- You must have two different colors of vegetables.
- Baking soda is just as good as toothpaste.
- Soda pop is just colored water.
- Scooters are bad; they wear out one shoe.
- If you get a BB gun, somebody will lose an eye.
- We can go from here to Hartford and back on the smell (of gas in the tank).
- I've got plenty (of gas).
- Lemmings rush to the sea and commit suicide.
- The Grand Canyon resulted from water flowing over millions upon millions of years.

I could expound on each of these, but I'll only comment here on the source of energy. If all energy indeed comes to Earth from the sun, there would be no visible stars in the heavens for us to see at night. That energy summary statement was made in my elementary school classes by many teachers. Being a cooperative, docile student, I just shrugged it off. But my common sense told me that my teachers were misinformed. Moreover, the vast majority had zero powers of observation. I didn't take them nor school seriously.

Some Foundational Roots of Dumb Dickie

I FEEL BLESSED to have recovered a collection of family-related letters written during World War II. The letters were mostly between my Uncle Walter J. Klein and his betrothed, Rita Marie Lavery. Rita by marriage then became my Aunt Rita. I am grateful that Uncle Walter was a packrat.

One letter, dated Tuesday, May 4, 1943, was written to Walter by my mother Ellen Klein.

235 Reed St.
Stratford, Conn.
May 4, 1943

Dear Walt,

When I say that things happen around here I'm really not kidding. It seems that while we were down in Westport Sunday Emma started labor pains. She was all alone, so she crawled over to old Mr. Burke that owns the house, and asked him to get her an ambulance. He managed that somehow, and Emma had a 1 ½ lb. boy, who died after a few hours. It is very rarely that babies that small ever manage to survive.

If we had any sense at all, we would have been prepared for this, for she has come down at 7 months before, but she seemed to be feeling pretty good so far. In a way it is not the worst thing that could happen.

At least Emma is alright, and it wouldn't have been too easy for her to take care of another baby. She has her hands full as it is.

Ruth is staying home from school to take care of the smaller ones, and even if they aren't eating quite the way they are accustomed to, she manages with a helping hand here and there. I'm just wondering how gracefully Gus is going to go through this. He has to do a good deal of the housework now, and that isn't really up his alley.

The paper hangers are finally here, and by the end of the week some of the work ought to be out of the way at least. The sidewalks are also under construction up the other end of the street, and in a few days we ought to have that in, too.

The - - furnace just won't seem to go. It was pretty hot here last night, so I slowed the thing down to a walk. Well, it slowed down alright, and now it just seems to have decided that we don't need it any more and resists all advances with the dogged stubbornness of a mule.

Seems that I had the type of boat all bowled up. It belongs to the "lightning" class, whatever that means. Till I get to know a little more about boats it is just a name – speaking of names, maybe you could think of an appropriate one for it. It's light blue and white. (This is almost as bad as naming a baby.) It's got to be something light, frivolous and odd. That's a big order, but there must be an answer somewhere.

How are you doing with your marksmanship? Or are you on something else now? And you still haven't told me whether there are any bears up there. If there are I think we'll come up and bag one to take home for a pet. I was just dreaming of one the other night. A nice big black one that come up to give me a friendly hug. Crazy? But definitely. Write soon. I'll keep you posted if anything new turns up – which it no doubt will.

Ellen

As the grown son of Ellen Klein, I struggle now 75 years after the letter was written. It is hard for me to grasp the enormity of the events described as well as the mindset of my mother. I could write a treatise just trying to make sense of my mother's words.

I will make some abbreviated observations in this book. I'll start off by introducing the persons discussed. Walter was my father's younger brother. Walter was stationed at Fort Devens in the Berkshires, near Springfield, Massachusetts. Emma was Emma Lydia Klein Birk, sister to Walter and my father Albert Klein. Gus was Gustave "Gus" Birk, married to Emma. Gus was not the nicest and kindest person in the world. He was an alcoholic and otherwise poor husband and father. Ruth was Emma's oldest daughter, then age 14. Gus and Emma rented the first floor in a house owned by an older man, Mr. Burke, no relation. Emma and Gus also had two other children, Dorothy then age 4, and Arlene then age 1. These two girls were the two little ones my mother referred to.

To add to the woes, Gus and Emma had few amenities. They had no telephone. Without access to a telephone, Emma couldn't just call for help. Old Mr. Burke lived in an adjoining rear room of the house.

Note also that Gus and Emma lived two doors away from my family. We lived at 235 Reed Street. Gus and Emma lived at 209 Reed Street.

What shocks me was my mother's obvious disregard for human life. In her letter, she coldly said that at least Emma doesn't have another baby to care for. I again assert my claim—my mother Ellen Klein was cold and hard. She never loved any child, not even one of her own. Children were to her a burden and just another irksome chore to deal with. Children were no better than the weeds in the garden and the flies coming into the house.

Please note that Ellen devoted almost as much of the letter to her dilemma of coming up with a name for a recently purchased sailboat.

It's light blue and white. (This is almost as bad as naming a baby.)

It's got to be something light, frivolous and odd. That's a big order, but there must be an answer somewhere.

Ellen lays out three requirements for a boat's name. She states, "light, frivolous, and odd." In a prior comment, she declared that having to name a baby is a worse burden. She never suggests that any joy is associated with a child and selecting a name for the child. There is no hint that children are blessed and are treasured gifts from God. In my view, what my mother does not say speaks volumes—a thundering roar.

Ellen's discussion of bagging a black bear in the Berkshires to take home for a pet just floors me. Mother was obviously starved for love and affection, but yet she gives none to those close to her.

My granddaughter-in-law Jessica Tatko typed the collection of WWII letters, including the Ellen letter. Jessica remarked that she sees indications of attention deficit disorder. I tend to agree. Please note, neither Jessica nor I have professional training. We are not qualified to make a diagnosis. As lay people we can only wonder.

I am pleased to report that the collection of WWII courtship letters is now published and available: *Kisses When I Get Home,* Richard E. Klein, editor, 2019.

I trust that the reader will have found the Ellen letter and its discussion insightful. It is now time to move on to Dumb Dickie.

In telling the various Dumb Dickie escapades, I have roughly placed them in chronological order. Several themes reappeared in the process of recounting my memories, especially during my early life and formative years.

One theme is that I, Dickie Klein, had a guardian angel who was busy at work—a guardian angel who most certainly had been getting good annual bonuses. Dear reader, I wish to introduce you to Herman. I've given my guardian angel a masculine name and at times I use the pronoun "he." Angels aren't human and have no gender, but I use the masculine gender to make things easier for readers to grasp, as we are so accustomed to all humans having gender. Please accept my language usage or abuse thereof. I can attest that Herman has remained close to me for my entire life. I'd show you a photograph of him if I could, but I can't as Herman chooses to be invisible.

A second theme is that my mother was an intelligent woman, but her abundance of intelligence caused her to become overly immersed in all sorts of activities. Nurturing and caring for her children clearly were not top-of-the-list priorities. Her solution to her child-rearing obligations was to shoo my two older brothers and me out the door and for us to fend for ourselves.

I suppose that a third theme is that I have done some pretty dumb things in my lifetime.

When growing up during the WWII national wartime mobilization, my two older brothers and I had lots of time on our hands, so some mischief happened. I was told that Don, when little, amused himself by removing the gas cap on the family car, picking up bits of gravel from our driveway, and then dropping them, stone by stone, into the car's gas tank. Don, being a persistent kid, filled the gas tank until no more gravel would fit in. I don't recall the consequences for Donnie, but Pop had to remove the gas tank and empty out all the gravel.

And Now Comes Dumb Dickie

PERHAPS ONE OF THE DUMBEST THINGS I ever did related to Pop's 1934 Chevy coupe. When I was about five, I found some roofing nails in the garage. As kids we played with sticks, pretend swords, and all manner of pointed objects. Inspired by war images, such as a cartoon of a paratrooper coming down with his parachute, about to land on a pointed church steeple, I placed roofing nails standing upright behind and ahead of each of the four tires of the Chevy, which was parked in the driveway. When Pop tried to go somewhere, the car just settled to the ground; all four tires went flat at once. Don then blurted out, "Dickie did it."

Pop spent the rest of the day repairing the four flat tires. Tires during WWII were scarce and almost impossible to obtain. Pop had no air compressor, so in addition to fixing each flat tire he had to pump up each one using a handpump. Every time Pop saw me that day I got another spanking. It was easy for him to find me since I was on the living room sofa still crying from the last spanking. It proved to be an unhappy day for me.

My mother was one to do her shopping daily. It was a part of her European upbringing and culture. Things like meat and dairy items had to be fresh as freezers were not a part of daily life in those days. Also, shopping for her was a social event. As she went from shop to shop, she would exchange small talk with the merchants and storekeepers, each of whom she knew by name. At other times she would make a stop at the post office or pay a utility bill.

One day when I was about five or six, as she was preparing to get into the car to do her errands, I asked if I could go along.

"No," was her resounding answer. The practice was that I would be left home alone, as my two older brothers were in school.

Being very young, foolish, and yet resourceful, I decided to go anyway. My remedy was to jump onto the car's back bumper. Her car was the family's 1941 Dodge sedan. The Dodge, like many cars of that era, had a firm bumper. It also had two vertical bumper guards, spaced sufficiently apart so that the trunk lid could be opened.

I sat facing backwards on the back bumper, straddling the bumper guard on the driver's side, feet dangling out behind.

Mother had no idea I was there. She backed out of the driveway, then accelerated and drove off. When she turned from Wakelee Avenue onto Main Street, I can recall the car really picking up speed. She was soon going 30 or 35 MPH. I didn't fall off because I was able to hold on to the top of the bumper guard much like a saddle horn.

Fortunately for me, Mother ended her trip by pulling into diagonal parking at the nearby Paradise Green shopping center. Once the car came to a stop, she got out and headed to her first shopping errand. I jumped off and ran onto the sidewalk to greet my unsuspecting mother. Of course, she was surprised to see me, but nothing much was said. Only years later did I conclude that she must have thought I'd hitched a ride in the back seat and hidden myself on the floor. She never realized I had been precariously dangling on the car's back bumper.

I wish to express my sincere thanks to Herman, my guardian angel.

In kindergarten, one activity during our half-day session was to play store. Each time we played store, somebody was chosen to be the storekeeper. When it got to be my turn, I did great except for one detail that I overlooked. I was so excited to be the storekeeper that I forgot to actually take in any play money as I responded to customer requests for stuff. I literally gave the store away. Nobody really noticed or cared, but I later felt an emptiness as I had my chance and forgot to collect any play money. This was just the beginning of my stupidity with money.

When enrolled in kindergarten, I noticed an amazing thing: a girl sitting at the table diagonally across from me. She had blonde hair in curls. She was absolutely beautiful. Somehow, up until then, I knew that girls existed, but nothing of this order. For me, it was so painful to look at her, I chose to not look her way. I just wasn't prepared, so it was easier to avoid even looking.

After a few years went by, I found out more about her. In about second grade, I ventured onto the street where she lived. I got close enough to her house that I could see the house number: 72.

I decided to tell her that I loved her. I wrote her a brief letter. In fact, it was very brief. I knew her name and initials but didn't know how to spell her name. The letter was simply, "Dear G.L., I love you."

I was too shy to sign the letter. I put a stamp on the envelope with the unsigned letter inside. It was addressed to G.L., 72 XYZ Street, Stratford, Connecticut. I also neglected to add a return address. That was my first stab at real romance. I never got a reply.

Gail graduated with me from high school. She remained a beauty and knockout. All throughout her school years, she was admired and respected. She was polite, friendly, very intelligent, and social. She was a cheerleader and the majorette of the high school marching band. Many years later at a high school class reunion, I recounted to her how enamored I was with her in kindergarten. I got a warm hug in return. She recounted how her mother went to such extremes to curl her hair and make her attractive, as if she was a princess.

In first grade I was seated at my table. The activity was some form of reading. Our teacher then told us to return our reading books to the designated shelf. I decided instead to sit on my book. Clearly, I was not doing as told. The teacher, Mrs. Eursham, an old battle axe if one ever existed, spotted the book. I was sternly reprimanded. As I recall, the chair had a contour, so the book had become deformed as I sat on it. In addition to the reprimand, I was demoted to a lower level reading group.

This next story isn't so much about a dumb mistake, but instead about dumb thinking. I can't even recall my age when this happened, but I'll assume I was around five or six. While in the family car we passed a street construction site in Bridgeport on Stratford Avenue. The location was close to the Bridgeport-Stratford town line. Workers had dug a huge excavation in the street's pavement. I recall seeing a crane with the boom positioned over the massive hole. What was amazing to me was that a cart, or compressor, or possibly a small cement mixer had been lifted up by the crane, and was thus suspended in the air high above the excavation.

My immediate assumption was that the two-wheeled whatever was lifted so as to be buried under the street and covered over with asphalt. A comic strip popular at the time was called the Toonerville Trolley, which depicted an awkward, top-heavy trolley with little wheels. As a kid it was difficult for me to separate reality and comic strip images, so I wondered if indeed the thing being buried was the Toonerville Trolley. For several years, whenever I passed by that site I continued to reflect on the buried cement mixer, or Toonerville Trolley, or whatever.

As an historical note, the mythical place Toonerville was associated with the poverty of the 1930s Great Depression. Poor people lived in a simple and desolate outskirts town just trying to survive. The image of Toonerville became the basis of a cartoon strip. These types of cartoons allowed people to just have a laugh. Transportation in Toonerville was provided by a trolley which was more cartoon than real.

The sketch above depicts the Toonerville Trolley.

As a kid it was my trait not to ask questions, but instead to ponder the world and figure out its logic using my own reasoning, even though my reasoning often came up with incorrect conclusions. Whenever I would ask a question of my family about the why of something, I commonly expected to be ridiculed. Hence, I became conditioned to not ask questions.

Burying a cement mixer just didn't make sense. It wasn't until well into my adulthood that I finally understood what I had seen as a kid. Upon the close of the work day, it was and still is routine for work crews to hook small equipment at a job site onto a crane, hoist it way up in the air, and position the crane arm so as to make the item less available for theft or vandalism. In hindsight the mixer being hung up in the sky makes perfect sense, but as a kid I was puzzled. I had rushed to a conclusion without really having all the facts. This was to become a pattern.

One cold wintery night Mother came into our (the boys') bedroom. It was axiomatic that we slept with the windows open, typically about nine inches. Also, windows had to be open on two sides of the bedroom to allow for cross ventilation. Mother insisted that inside air was bad and that healthy living resulted from breathing fresh air. It was bitterly cold that night.

"Do you want a quilt?" she asked me. I was already in bed but not yet asleep.

I had no clue what the word "quilt" meant. The fact that the word started with a Q was strange to my sense of language at the time. I immediately envisioned some form of straitjacket contraption that I would have been zipped and locked into. Mother had a history of pulling out all sorts of surprises, at least in my mind. I wasn't interested, and I wasn't buying.

"No, thanks." I replied.

I froze that night in bed, as I had only an ordinary blanket. My role as the little brother was to be forever belittled. No matter what, I would suffer in silence as opposed to ever asking for help or admitting that I was freezing.

In about the first or second grade my mother decided I

would wear a pair of suspenders to school. There was no out. Mother made me wear them. I thought they were dorky-looking. After leaving the house, as I walked to school I rearranged my garments to cover up the suspenders, putting them under my shirt. The problem was that I couldn't figure out how to tuck my shirt in.

In about second grade, my cousin Dorothy (1939-2009) and I started to walk together to Paradise Green, the local shopping center. On the way, we met another neighborhood kid, Freddie Nelson. I wanted to be with Freddie, so I told Dorothy I was going with him. To this day, the idea that I deserted my own cousin to run off with another kid brings shame and disgrace to me. I am truly sorry.

One time when I was in second grade, as best I can recall, I was playing with an older neighborhood kid named Earl Killdorf. We were on an embankment, about 20 feet above East Main Street in Stratford. There was a typical New England stone wall running along the top of the embankment. Soon we were pushing the stones off and watching them tumble down the embankment and roll onto East Main Street.

After we had rolled down, say, 20 or 30 rocks, a police car pulled up and stopped.

The sketch above depicts a Stratford police car *circa* 1946. The Stratford police cars back then were entirely black, with black tires. To my memory, the Stratford police cars had a single red light on top. The police cars were referred to as cherry tops. The siren was mounted on a front fender. When the police car showed up that day, it had approached without the fanfare of flashing lights and sirens. The policeman got out of his car. He didn't chase after us. Earl and I didn't run, instead hunching down and hiding behind the stone wall. The policeman waved for us to come down, which we did. He took our names and addresses and did whatever police do in such circumstances. I have no memory of how the roadway was cleared of the stones. After walking home, I dreaded the thought that the police would come to my home to talk to my parents. Later that day, I did see the black police cruiser with its cherry top parked in front of Killdorf's house.

Fortunately for me, the police cruiser never came to my house. I guess that because Killdorf was older than me, by perhaps three years, the Stratford cop focused on him as the instigator and culprit. In those days, the last thing any kid wanted was for the police to come to talk to the parents because that would have meant some real punishment.

I have never told anybody about this story until this writing, some 70 years after the fact. I don't know whatever happened to Earl Killdorf. He soon moved away. I don't remember ever playing with him other than that one time.

***

Mother's cooking had two characteristics: commonality of menu and vastly overcooked vegetables. One day she cooked cabbage that was as dismal as could ever be possible. The ground rule in the Klein house was that one had to eat the vegetables. Again, there was no out. Somehow the idea came to me to sprinkle some cinnamon on the overcooked cabbage. I so despised the taste of the bland cabbage that I proceeded to sprinkle on cinnamon lavishly, perhaps $1/8^{th}$ of an inch in thickness.

I ate it and survived.

The outcome was an overdose of cinnamon, to the point that even today, some 70 years later I can't tolerate the taste of cinnamon.

As an aside, once in my adult life I recounted the cinnamon story to my mother. She told me then about a similar experience of hers. When she first arrived in America in 1926, she overdosed on ice cream. Ice cream had been very rare back in Denmark. She told me that following her overdose, ice cream never appealed to her again.

***

A common social event in my childhood was a picnic. Once the family went to a large picnic organized by some Danish society. These organizations were social, fraternal, and dedicated to providing benefits such as life insurance policies. The picnic was held at a grove along North Main Street in Bridgeport. While there, I got a hot dog and prepared to eat it. A few older guys, and I do mean old guys, remarked, "Hey kid, you're eating your hot dog wrong."

Each time I would position it differently so as to take a bite, they continued to badger me about eating the hot dog incorrectly. Do you bite one end? Do you stick it in your mouth aiming it directly at your mouth? Do you bite it in the middle? Whatever I did was wrong.

Those old geezers really got me flustered. I must have been six or seven at the time. I was confused. They were having a great time pulling my leg. It was years later that I figured out there is no wrong way to eat a hot dog, short of dropping it on the ground. So long as you can take bites and chew, it has to be the best way to eat it. As an adult, I take note whenever I see old guys ganging up on a little kid. People who have so little else to do in life other than tease young children are pretty poor excuses for manhood.

⸻

As the youngest of three boys, I wore hand-me-down clothes. When Donald outgrew his clothing, Freddie wore it next, and I was third in line.

During WWII certain materials, such as buttons, became scarce. Buttons required a supply of plastic, which came from petroleum, which in turn was scarce.

When I was in about second grade, I inherited a pair of pants that had cardboard buttons on the fly. The war was over but the pants with cardboard buttons were still there for me to wear to school. Zippers as we are now accustomed to did not yet exist, at least in terms of our clothing.

Because pants were washed in the laundry over and over again, by the time I got to wear those hand-me-down pants, the cardboard buttons had become frayed. This made unbuttoning—and rebuttoning—near impossible for my small fingers. That was quite embarrassing for me.

When I was in third grade (or thereabouts), the Town of Stratford started a major upgrade of its sewage system. Streets were dug up and sewers were installed. On Wakelee Avenue at the base of a hill, the project included construction of a large manhole made of bricks and mortar. This sewer project was on the same route that I used to walk to and from school. It became my habit to stop and observe the progress daily, even several times a day. Once, a dump truck came with its back end filled with a load of bricks. To my utter shock, the truck driver raised the hoist of the truck, dumping the pile of bricks onto the pavement.

R KLEIN
2016

My shock was rooted in the fact that some of the bricks cracked or were broken as a result. Based on my upbringing, you just didn't whimsically break things. Things like bricks cost money, so you never break anything as that was a violation of a cardinal rule. In the Klein household, only material things mattered. The expenditure of time was not a consideration.

For years I pondered those events and all the wasted and broken bricks. As I grew into adulthood the answer came to me. It would have cost more in labor to unload the bricks by hand compared to the value of the bricks that were destroyed. Also, masons commonly use and even need broken or half bricks in a bricklaying project. A third factor to bear in mind was the disruption to the flow of traffic. Dumping the bricks saved time. That saved time allowed Wakelee Avenue to get back to carrying normal traffic.

R KLEIN 2016

When the manhole was being constructed, it was widest at its base. The first layer of bricks rested on a poured concrete footing. As the upper layers of bricks were added, fewer bricks were used, causing the manhole to become narrower (tapered) at the top. Once construction of the manhole was completed, dirt was backfilled up against the exterior of the manhole. At the top, a cast iron access grate was installed. As each layer was laid, the brick mason needed half or broken bricks.

As kids, my brother Freddie and I both had marble collections. In playing marbles, the winner got to keep the loser's marble. Depending upon clarity and color, some marbles were vastly more desired than plain old marbles. Freddie was a pretty good marble shooter and so his collection was much bigger than mine. It was so large that it filled a massive cookie jar and must have been the equivalent of several gallons of marbles. My collection, if you want to call it that, was much smaller in comparison. And it got smaller yet.

Two boys playing marbles.

As I recall, the field of play had a center hole the size of a cup or slightly larger, and an outer ring that marked the playing field as well as the starting point.

It was common that kids on the school ground would play the game simply called marbles. The small hole or cup-sized recession was in the center of an open area of dirt, which was about five feet in diameter. The dirt surface was devoid of grass. The object was to somehow flick a marble, using one's thumbnail, to cause it to hit an opponent's marble. If the hit marble went into the hole, then the player hitting it got to keep the other player's marble. I don't recall the exact details, but a poor player could lose his marbles. Hence the expression came into usage, "losing all your marbles."

I happened to have a few incredibly clear and valuable marbles. I was stupid enough to play a game of marbles using them, and I lost my marbles. A lost marble is a lost marble. There was no consideration that it was a valuable or clear marble. It was pretty dumb of me to play a game of marbles where I played with valuable marbles when the other kid was only risking drab and cheap ones.

———

As kids, my two older brothers and I spent many Saturdays caddying. Our father Albert Klein, or Pop as we called him, had become an angry person to be around. We came to dread the coming of a Saturday because that meant being exposed to Pop's sharp tongue. My brothers and I had one mission on Saturdays: to get out of the house and thus away from Pop's angry demeanor. To aid our exodus, Pop also said, "Go out and make a buck." The obvious place to go was the Mill River Country Club, in nearby north Stratford. In those days, kids from blue-collar families worked as caddies for wealthier white-collar types.

Golf is a gentlemen's game, a game where rules, honesty, and etiquette are foremost. I understood that my role was to carry a bag of golf clubs, but I was not to speak unless spoken to.

Over the years, I noticed that some kids got generous tips—but never me. It wasn't until much later in life that I understood why I never got tips. I believed in altruism and fairness. In playing golf, at times a ball would end up in what was called "the rough." The rules of golf dictated that if a ball was not able to be played, the golfer had to play from a new location but after incurring a penalty stroke. When any golfer lost a ball, the entire foursome and caddies would fan out in search of the lost ball.

If I ever was the person finding the ball, I treated the found ball with reverence. I'd point out, "Oh, here it is down in this gopher hole" or in some other impossible position. Unknown to me at the time, the less ethical caddies would discreetly move the ball to a better position or "lie." After the ball was given some assistance, then and only then did the caddy announce, "Oh, here it is."

In those days, golfers commonly bet a dollar a hole. The winning low score on each hole later settled up. The winning golfer got the wager pay-offs as well as the ego boost of out-playing his rivals. The winning golfer was prone to being generous at tip time.

At the time, I never realized that my honesty was to blame for my lack of tips.

The Korean War started on June 25, 1950. President Harry Truman sent American troops into Korea to fight what was described as a police action. War was never declared by Congress, but the name Korean War sticks in most minds. I was 11 years old at the war's start. Each day the local newspaper showed a front-cover map of our shrinking defensive perimeter at the port city of Pusan. As an idealist who believed in America, I was crushed. A bunch of ragtag Commies wearing pajamas were humiliating America. General Douglas MacArthur changed all that. On September 15, 1950, our forces did a naval landing at Inchon. That spectacular landing, against all odds, turned the tide of war strongly in our favor.

In late 1950, massive hordes of Chinese crossed over the Yalu River. A stalemate followed. America lacked the will to fight. Korea and North Korea to this day remain a problem.

To understand Dumb Dickie, it is insightful to first understand how the Korean War shaped me. I was deeply altered and influenced by the Korean War.

I am a crushed idealist. That is what caused me to become a cynic. As a second and critical aspect, I conduct my life with Inchon as my thought process model. I seek to avoid long, drawn-out conflicts and irksome tasks. Instead, I seek challenges and problem areas where I can perform one masterful invasion—and come out victorious on high ground. In the conduct of my battles, I prefer to win with little effort, not even working up a sweat.

I'm getting ahead of myself, but I want to comment on my doctoral dissertation in mechanical engineering. I never conducted an experiment. I never wrote a computer program. I never ran any computer programs, crunching out numbers. Instead, I stated and proved two theorems related to the problem of how to measure the movements in things that wiggle and flex. My dissertation was expressed in fewer than 100 pages. I was in the door and out in three short years. This is far shorter and faster than your run of the mill dissertation in modern mechanical engineering.

The photograph above shows, from left to right, my father Albert Klein, brother Freddie, myself (Richard, a.k.a. Dumb Dickie), and brother Donald. The photograph was taken on Easter Sunday, April 9, 1950.

As I reflect back on my upbringing, I was never close to my father. I can't ever remember him playing ball with me, or taking the time to teach me in the finer ways of life. Pop had a fixation on survival. The survival of his sons was central to him. He didn't want my brothers and me to do anything dumb. I want to tell a story about one of the few times Pop tried to give us some advice. He wanted us to know how to properly jump onto a moving freight train.

Pop insisted on telling us how to execute this skill. The trick was to run alongside the boxcar and jump up and grab the ladder. In this discussion, it was assumed that the freight train was going faster than running speed. According to Pop, it was crucial to never go for the back ladder. Always go for the front ladder. If you try for the back ladder and miss, you will fall between the cars and get cut in half. In the case of the front ladder, the worst outcome will be that you will bounce against the side of the car and be thrown clear.

I don't recall a specific quote by Pop on this topic. I did get the sense that one of Pop's high school chums made the mistake of trying to grab the rear ladder.

When I was growing up, there was a man with no legs selling pencils on the sidewalk in downtown Bridgeport. Because the man had no legs, he sat on a small wooden board with casters. His tin can or jar of pencils would be on the sidewalk in front of him. His legs were cut off at mid-thigh, so he was about three feet tall. Pop never said that this man was his friend, but I just assumed the connection.

Kids love to brag. In my neighborhood various kids bragged about how early in the spring they had gone swimming. One kid claimed April. Perhaps another kid boasted about swimming in March. Who knows?

On a warm late February day, I was at Webb's Pond close to the Mill River Country Club in Stratford. I was alone and in a desolate location. Because it must have been in the seventies air temperature wise, I decided to go swimming. I took off all my clothes except for my underpants. I jumped in, off an embankment. Indeed, it was cold water! I got out quickly, but to me, I had been swimming in February. Having no towel along, I tried as best I could to dry myself off using my tee shirt as a pseudo-towel. I put my clothes back on except for the wet skivvies and the damp tee shirt. To this day I have never told anybody about swimming in February. I am not a person who brags about what I have done. Instead, in my inner being I have the satisfaction of knowing that whatever other people are claiming to have done, I have done that much or more. Nonetheless, it was a fairly dumb thing to go swimming in February, at least in Connecticut.

I once was playing with a BB gun. I wondered if it would hurt if I shot my foot. I aimed at the top of my foot, pointing down to the toes. Yes, it hurt.

I was once climbing in the trees behind our house. I wondered if it would hurt to jump down from a height of about twelve feet. Yes, it hurt.

Once when my brother Freddie and I were home alone, we decided to bake a cake. We followed a recipe, but we didn't understand the distinction between baking powder and baking soda. Things like t and T didn't register as they relate to teaspoons versus tablespoons. We obviously got some quantities wrong as well as some incorrect ingredients. The cake tasted terrible, but as I recall we ate it anyway.

I joined Boy Scout Troop 202 in the spring of 1950. I took to Scouting, advancing in rank and becoming confident with camping. With camping came outdoor cooking. I took note of an advertisement. "No soggy under-crust" proclaimed the advertisement for Morton's Chicken Pot Pie. I purchased one and took it camping. In my altruistic mind, I anticipated a chicken pot pie with a crisp and tasty under-crust. To my dismay, I discovered that my chicken pot pie had no under-crust at all. Without an under-crust, it certainly wasn't soggy.

When I was in about eighth grade, I became more adventurous. One of my traits was to find or even create a private space—a place where I could be away from the sight of my parents. In that era, I also found some lumber. I won't bother to define the word "found." I used the lumber to build a small pigeon coop. It was about 4'x4', and about that high as well. I even shingled its roof.

Yes, I had several pigeons at one point. The pigeons came from under the Washington Bridge over the Housatonic River between Stratford and Devon. I found baby pigeons in a nest under the bridge and raised them. Pigeons are another story, so I want to get back to private places.

My pigeon coop was in the backyard at Reed Street. I cut an opening in the floor to use as a door. This allowed me to start digging down. I dug down about six feet. Then I dug a side cavity. This was my private space where I could get away. I used a ladder to climb down and back up. As I recall, I used a candle for illumination.

In hindsight, it was incredibly dumb of me to dig a hole and seclude myself underground. It never occurred to me to use more wood for ceiling supports. The dirt above me could have collapsed and I would have never made it out, at least not alive and breathing.

After a rain, I discovered that my hidden cavern had in fact collapsed. The pigeon coop fell partially into the resulting muddy hole. Whatever I had stored down there was lost. I never made any attempt to re-dig the hole. Somehow, I managed to lift up and retrieve the pigeon coop. The access ladder was sticking up. I was able to retrieve the ladder by yanking it up by the exposed end. I filled the hole back in and life went on.

I have to thank Herman—my guardian angel—who I certainly kept busy.

As the world returned to peace following World War II, my mother wanted a family photograph to send to her cousins and other relatives in Denmark. During the five years of Nazi occupation of Denmark, from 1940 to 1945, sending and receiving letters didn't take place.

As was typical, when we took family photographs, we gathered on the lawn at home following church. That way, we were properly dressed. We also had spare time so nobody was in a hurry.

The problem was that my brother Freddie wasn't about to behave. When my father went to take the picture, Freddie stuck out his tongue. Dumb Dickie couldn't help but follow Freddie's lead. After all, he was my older brother. Finally, my mother said, "If that is how you want to be seen, so be it." Snap, my father took the picture. Yes, copies were mailed to relatives in Denmark. Donald, the oldest, was holding the family cat, Missy. Donald always had an affinity for pets.

Dumb Dickie (center), Freddie (right), Donald holding Missy, Mother (standing) letting it all slide.

Riding a bike became a big part of my life as I was growing up on Reed Street. The irony was that while I rode my bike virtually everywhere as a kid, I neglected to do one thing: develop the muscle memory to pedal correctly. Once when I was in my thirties, I went on a daylong bike ride of about 30 miles with two colleagues. My friends had derailleur-geared bikes, whereas I had an internally geared three-speed. As the trip went on, I got tired. It was agreed that I would trade bikes with a colleague. This change of bikes helped me recover. My friend's bike had toe clips, so for the first time ever I tried lifting up on my pedal as it came back around and up.

I had never previously used my leg muscles in that way. I realized that in addition to not ever having used toe clips, I consistently only pushed downward with my forward and down stroke. Because I didn't lift my rising leg, I was making use of only certain muscles—and not all available muscles. This story explains in part why I wasn't good at most sports. From the day I started to ride a bike, I retained less than optimal motor plans. My muscles should have learned to make adjustments from feedback received until they become efficient at a task. But for me, doing sports activities was always like doing it for the first time.

Grandmother Kamma would often give each of us kids a silver dollar in a fancy box for Christmas. I collected them for a while, but I soon discovered that candy stores accepted silver dollars in addition to paper money. In hindsight, the fool and his silver are soon parted.

Over the years Grandmother Kamma exchanged letters with her various Danish relatives, notably her siblings. Kamma tore off and saved the stamps from the letters, most from Denmark. She kept the stamps in a large box, about the size of a shoebox. One Christmas, she gave me a box full of such stamps. She knew I had become interested in stamp collecting. My words to her were, "Some of them are nice." That didn't go over well and was certainly undiplomatic.

My brothers and I are shown above. We were certainly a rough and tumble lot. Left to right are Dickie, Fred, and Donald. I would hazard a guess as to a date being in June of 1944. Our ages would be, respectively, five, six, and eight.

In the fall of 1949, Old Man Burke died. As a neighbor, he had owned the nearby house at 209 Reed Street. My Aunt Emma and her family rented the first floor. I was ten years old at the time. Following Old Man Burke's death, several ladies were busy clearing out the rear room where Burke had lived. Some people were marveling that Old Man Burke, although he lived a frugal existence, had money hidden away. The ladies were finding an occasional $5 or $10 bill hidden within.

Because Burke had kept a large garden, the ladies handed out some garden produce to the neighborhood kids standing around. I was handed a squash.

I was delighted to say the least. Immediately, I had a plan. I would go out that night after supper and play a trick or treat on somebody. To be more precise, the treat part wasn't even envisioned. It was going to be all trick. As kids, we knew which neighbors to target, as certain neighbors had reputations for being grumps. I was already picturing Bobby Johnson's father's house. I imagined smashing the squash on the front doorstep, ringing the doorbell and running away. Of course, I had to wait for darkness following supper.

My family always ate supper at 6:10. That's how regular we were in that kind of thing. Pop usually returned home from work at about 5:30. He would wash and possibly scan the newspaper. The power plant's whistle blew at 6:00. We sat down. Pop wasn't a religious or spiritual man. His usual words were, "We're all set." We ate at 6:10, just like clockwork.

That night I was shocked to see cooked squash for supper. I was crushed. The pill was bitter. Not only was my majestic Halloween trick smashed, I had to eat squash for supper.

A favorite Saturday pastime was to go hiking. Often it was just my brother Freddie and me. At times Freddie Nelson, a neighborhood kid, came along as well. Our usual destination was the river road up along the Housatonic River. On these day-long hikes we would commonly bring some food for lunch, and of course something to drink. Our stuff was usually carried in a small knapsack.

On one such hike the drink was soda pop, which came in glass bottles. The idea of soda in cans had not yet happened; beverage cans with tear-off tabs didn't exist. The problem was that we forgot to bring a bottle opener. When you are dying of thirst, soda in a bottle doesn't do much good if you can't open the bottle. I'm sure we tried everything conceivable, such as our belt buckles, but the soda pop cap wouldn't come off. In the end, in a desperate move, I recall hitting the bottle's neck against a concrete bridge rail. The neck of the bottle broke off.

I was able to fit the bottle's jagged glass neck into my mouth by opening my mouth wide. I was able to drink most of the soda. I did worry about swallowing some broken glass, so I played it safe. I left an inch or so of soda still in the bottom of the bottle. I appear to have lived as opposed to dying of internal bleeding. Nonetheless, drinking directly from the broken neck of a glass bottle has to be classified as pretty dumb.

In my later accumulation of wisdom and worldly tricks, I now know that one can usually remove a cap on a bottle by having a sharp edge, such as a railing on a bridge or even a sharp edge of concrete. One places the cap's edge on an opposing edge. Then one pushes the bottle down. In later years once I had a car, the problem of opening a bottle became easier. I would open the car door and use the protruding door hinge and door post as a fulcrum to pop off a bottle cap.

The sketch above shows a common beer can and bottle opener. In that post-WWII era, the scarce bottle openers were highly coveted. Recall the 1967 movie *Cool Hand Luke* as Luke, in his drunken stupor, wears a bottle opener hanging around his neck

I once decided to play hooky. My difficulty was in not fully understanding the rules. For those who don't know the phrase, playing hooky means to skip school. I was in ninth grade at Wooster Junior High in Stratford. Mother was away, Pop was off somewhere on a job for Bullard's, and my oldest brother Don was already in college at UVM in Burlington, Vermont, so Freddie and I were left home alone. With both parents gone, I decided to just stay home, mostly resting in bed.

As the day went on, I encountered two problems. First was that the school office called home to verify with my parents that I was ill or whatever. The phone rang. I opted to ignore it. In hindsight, that was a mistake. Friends who were better at playing hooky later told me that I should have answered the phone. I should have told the school office that I was sick and that my mother was momentarily out shopping. Then the second problem arose. To my surprise, my mother came home in the afternoon, a day earlier than I had anticipated. I heard her downstairs, so I opted to hide in the small attic next to my bedroom. I was hoping to run the clock out. Soon, the phone rang again. Mother answered. After a short conversation, she hung up and came upstairs to my bedroom, obviously looking for me. She didn't find me. She went downstairs. I soon had to face the music, so I got out of hiding and came downstairs. I tried to look sick and weak. My mother accepted the story, or at least didn't confront me. I stated that I was not feeling well. Somehow the day passed, though I can't say it was a particularly fun day of hooky.

If one is to play a game, it is important to understand the game and follow its rules.

When I was about 13, I became interested in model electric trains. I had the Lionel train set. The other popular brand was

American Flyer. As I purchased more track and a pair of switches with spare money, I decided to screw the track layout onto a plywood sheet that would slide under my bed. After purchasing some plywood, I took a saw and cut it down to size so that it would slide under my bed. Next, I went to screw the track on. To my surprise, I had cut the plywood too small, and so I was not able to make the track fit as I had intended. I had cut the plywood by eye and didn't measure first. If I had measured the distance between the bed legs and also laid out the track requirements before cutting, I could have better cut the plywood so the track would fit on the plywood while still fitting under the bed.

I never mounted the train track onto plywood. I learned to measure three times, cut once. My dumb mistake was in cutting without doing any measurements first.

When I was about 14, I was working with Pop's engine lathe in the basement. I had made a miniature cannon out of brass. It was about two or three inches long overall. It actually looked pretty nice as it had side mounts and toy wheels. The barrel had been bored out with a drill bit mounted in the lathe's tailstock. The cannon's bore was about 5/16th's of an inch in inside diameter. When I first built the scale model cannon, my objective was to just have it to look at. But once it was finished, I got the idea of test firing it.

I got some black powder by cutting apart some firecrackers. I drilled a small hole in the upper back of the cannon in which to insert a firecracker fuse. At least this is how they shot off cannons in the movies. After pouring in the black powder, I rammed in a lead ball, probably a spherical fishing weight or sinker, as my projectile. I lit the fuse and stood back. The fuse went out after burning down to the brass cannon's shell.

So as not to waste the effort, I then heated a thin steel wire with a match. I had seen that done in the movies also. I held onto the hot wire with a pair of pliers. I pushed the tip end of the hot wire down into the firing hole. That was successful. The cannon did shoot, but it also exploded, splitting the brass cannon completely into two halves. I had positioned the cannon on the basement floor for firing, and so was within reaching distance, hunched down, when it exploded. I ended up being knocked over backwards on my rear. It proved that I knew very little about gunsmithing and the different tensile strength properties of various metals. Brass is pretty and easy to machine but please note that few successful gun manufacturers sell guns with brass barrels.

The lead bullet impacted a piece of plywood I had set in front of the cannon, leaning against the basement wall. The impact made a fairly deep hole in the plywood, about ½ inch.

The brass cannon exploded with me in close proximity. I was sore from falling over on my rear, but other than a bruise and a surprise, my guardian angel Herman had protected me.

When I was 15, in the fall of 1954, four of us went squirrel hunting. The three guys with me were my brother Freddie, John Ibold, and Ned Coutant. They were all older than me. As such, the three of them had shotguns and hunting licenses. I couldn't get a hunting license as I was still just 15, and so I didn't carry a gun.

The area was public land, a state forest in Eastern Connecticut. Being legal was important. As the four of us were walking in the woods along an old logging trail, someone spotted a squirrel going into a hole in a large tree. The hole was about 25 feet above the ground. As I had no gun, I offered to bang on the tree's trunk with a rock. I went about 20 or possibly 25 feet into the tangled brush to the base of the tree. I picked up a nearby hefty rock. Connecticut forests had no shortage of rocks. I then stepped up to the tree and hit it. Instantly the squirrel exited. It turns out the species was a flying squirrel.

Above is shown my granddaughter Anna's sketch of a Northern Flying Squirrel. Its range covers mostly the northern half of North America, but extends down to include Connecticut. It doesn't fly *per se* but instead has an extended glide. When the legs are stretched out, the skin makes the equivalent of a wing or lifting surface.

The flying squirrel dove straight down, directly between the three hunters and my position at the base of the tree. As the airborne squirrel approached the hunters, Freddie aimed and leveled his shotgun. At point blank range Freddie pulled the trigger. The gun was Pop's 12-gauge duck hunting shotgun, full choke.

The problem was that I was directly in the line of fire—and at close range, about 20 feet in front of Freddie.

Yes, Freddie shot me.

God works in mysterious ways. Persons shot at a close range from a 12-gauge shotgun commonly suffer fatal wounds. The tissue damage combined with profuse bleeding are often massive. The only thing that saved my life was that I had previously stepped behind the tree trunk. Herman had planted a thorny bramble bush on the tree's front side, so it was easier for me to step around to the tree's far side. The large tree trunk absorbed the brunt of the shotgun's blast and saved my life. Freddie couldn't see me because of the undergrowth, mostly leaves. Being naïve, I had assumed that the gunfire would be well over my head. At the time I didn't have the slightest concern for my safety. Leaves and light foliage do little in stopping a massive discharge of shotgun pellets, especially at close range. The tree trunk, about 24 inches in diameter, fortuitously absorbed all the pellets except one.

That one pellet struck me in the boot, near my right ankle. My stance had been such that only a portion of my lower right foot was unprotected.

Getting shot is a strange experience. Your body senses that something has gone wrong, but you don't quite know for certain. I am certain however that a few well-defined swear words departed from my lips.

After I made my way back to the three guys, we decided to check my body for more pellet wounds. I stripped bare naked. We searched my body but fortunately didn't find any additional pellet wounds. After putting my clothes back on and after we dug out the one pellet with the point of a hunting knife, I opted to walk back to the car. As I recall, even with three shotguns up, aimed, and ready to shoot, the squirrel escaped getting hit. Ned, John, and Freddie had all fired virtually simultaneously as the squirrel sprang from its hole. Freddie had Pop's old Ranger pump repeater, so it was Freddie who got off the fourth shot—aimed directly at me. I did recognize in later life the value of being very selective in agreeing to go hunting with others.

As an editorial note, I have characterized this incident of getting shot by Freddie as a near death or close encounter experience. If the bramble bush had not been where it was, I would have taken the full brunt of Freddie's shotgun discharge. I have had perhaps a dozen or so such close encounters with death over the years, being saved by the thinnest of chances. And Herman.

My brother Fred and I went into Capital Loan, a pawn shop in Bridgeport. I was 15 at the time. Fred was 16. We were looking at a used .30-30 lever-action deer rifle. Fred and I assumed no store would sell guns to us at our young age.

"Are you the sons of Al Klein?" the shop owner asked.

"Yes," we answered.

He sold us the rifle.

In those days (*circa* 1954) there was no paperwork on long-gun purchases. He made out a simple receipt, we paid in cash, and that was the end of it. Because we were the sons of Al Klein, he would have sold us virtually anything in the store, excepting handguns. My assumption was that the pawnbroker and Pop were friends from their grade-school days in Stratford.

Some Car Stories

SOON AFTER I purchased my first car, a 1936 Plymouth, for $10, I got to feeling pretty much on top of the world. One day I was stopped at Pjura's Sunoco Service on North Main Street in Stratford. I stopped there frequently because my close friend Harry Wilcoxson worked there pumping gas. It happened that a fire truck with all its lights and sirens blaring passed us, headed north on Main Street. I jumped into my Plymouth and decided to follow the action. I hastily pulled out and started to chase after the fire truck, or at least go that way. The problem was that I had pulled out directly in front of a cop car that was responding to the emergency. Once I saw the police car's flashing lights behind me I pulled over. The police car had other places to go, so he went on by. I assumed, however, that he would search for me after the fire emergency had settled down. My problem was that the cop would be looking for a light gray 1936 Plymouth four-door sedan.

I decided to change all that.

Several hours and a can of black paint later, I had painted the Plymouth black. I also removed my shiny hubcaps, replacing them with the original Plymouth hubcaps. Yes indeed, in my teenage years, hubcaps were a big deal. After completing this cosmetic refurbishing, the car looked pretty different and yet good.

The cops never found me. Or maybe I wasn't even on their radar screen.

The above photographs show my 1936 Plymouth, when it was still painted light gray. In the first photograph, the four people, from left to right, are Paul Shirra, LeRoy Cebik, Richard (Dickie) Klein, and Freddie Ashcroft. The second photograph shows a frontal view.

At this point I want to inject the story as to how I came to buy that car. An elderly gentleman, George Bushane, owned that car. He was a regular customer at Racine's Sunoco, where I worked. Mr. Bushane had purchased that car new in 1936. He was sixty-six at the time. Now think of this—George Bushane was born in 1870, only five years after the civil war ended. That was also six years before Custer's Last Stand at Little Big Horn. He would have been at or even beyond draft age to serve in the Spanish-American War in 1898.

George Bushane bought a new car in 1936 because his children were fighting to get his money. He decided to spend it instead. The problem was that he outlived the car. In 1956 he was 86 years old, when he then bought another car. The 1936 Plymouth wasn't running very well by then and so I was able to buy it for about the price of scrap metal. It turns out that all the Plymouth needed was a set of spark plugs and a simple tune-up. I had it running like a dream in short order.

George Bushane was a big man, so the driver's seat was collapsed from all his weight over the years. Somehow my body got used to it. He also smoked cigars, so I got used to the smell of cigar smoke.

I now want to tell a story about buying my first junkyard engine. In 1956 I was still driving my first car, the 1936 Plymouth four-door sedan. An older friend suggested that I could get more power if I installed a DeSoto "Spitfire" engine. I went to Murphy Auto Wrecking in Milford, Connecticut, on the Boston Post Road. I was a green kid, and no match for the likes of Murphy, as that is all he was ever called. Murphy ended up selling me a Dodge engine, not a DeSoto Spitfire engine. Murphy rattled off his guarantee, "No knocks, no cracks, won't burn oil."

I have since learned in life that such a guarantee means nothing. As an idealistic kid I assumed that Murphy had checked the engine out or otherwise knew its history before making his pronouncement. In hindsight, I realize that was Murphy's standard line for any of his junkyard engines. The next thing

Murphy said was that he would start the engine while still in the junkyard car so that I could hear it running. Because the junkyard car was blocked in that day by other junk cars, it wasn't readily accessible. Murphy told me to come back another day.

When I came back to hear it run and close the deal, his workers had already moved the car and, in addition, had already pulled the engine. Without motor mounts, a battery, and most of all a cooling system, it was no longer possible to hear the engine running. Murphy explained that getting a battery and coolant would be too difficult, but again he repeated his no knocks, no cracks, won't burn oil storyline. I was so dumb that I accepted it and paid him $25, the agreed-upon price. His wrecker then delivered the engine hanging by a chain on the back of the wrecker's boom. It was taken not to my home, but instead to the rural home of my friend William "Billy" F. Ashcroft (1939-2013). The engine was placed inside a shed at the Ashcroft home. As will become significant later, the shed had a wooden floor. I now had a junkyard engine but no longer had my $25.

My reason for fixating on and selecting that particular engine was its paint. Let me explain. Sears-Roebuck sold remanufactured engines back then that were painted blue. The engine I was looking at was obviously a Sears-Roebuck rebuilt engine. Because of the newness of the paint, I assumed that the engine was fairly new, thus with low miles. I presumed the car had been wrecked, as opposed to just being old.

As I started to look at the engine in Billy Ashcroft's shed, I found that the engine's crank wouldn't turn. I decided to investigate. I soon discovered why the seemingly good engine wouldn't turn: It had been the victim of sugar. For the uninformed, when somebody doesn't like somebody else, one form of attack is to pour a cup or two of sugar into their gas tank. The sugar will dissolve into the gas. When the car's engine is warm and running, the sugar will get mixed into the crankcase and with the many internal engine parts. Once the engine is shut off and cools down, the sugar recrystallizes. The engine becomes worthless since it won't turn. Essentially, the sugar causes the engine to freeze up solid.

Being naïve, I decided to take the engine entirely apart, wash each piece clean, and then reassemble the engine. I got partway along with disassembly when another thing happened. Upon removing the main bearing caps, the crankshaft didn't come out. Obviously, it was stuck in place because of the sugar. So, being foolish, I proceeded to lift the engine off the shed's wooden floor using an overhead chain hoist suspended from a beam. With the engine about two feet above the floor, I proceeded to get down on the floor to examine what was going on. I was prone on the floor. I was on my side, right side down. My right forearm was extended underneath the suspended engine.

This is hard to describe in words, but the crankshaft and flywheel assembly suddenly fell. My right forearm was directly underneath. As the flywheel and crankshaft assembly struck the wooden floor, it bounced. The initial point of impact cracked the floor planks. After the bounce, the assembly jumped sideways several inches. The next time the flywheel hit the floor it landed just to the right of my forearm, having jumped over—and thus to the other side of—my exposed arm.

The Dodge engine had a fluid drive system, so the weight of the crank and flywheel was massive as it had the additional weight of the torque converter as well. A total weight exceeding 100 pounds would not have been far off. Again, the drop distance was about two feet, so any impact by the sharp teeth on the flywheel's ring gear would have severed or severely crushed my arm.

I have previously commented on angels acting to protect us. It was only by the most miraculous of interventions that I still have my right hand. If my right hand had been a few more inches to one side or the other, it would have been crushed. I could have even bled to death as I was alone in the shed at the time, which was several hundred feet away from Billy's home. I have no idea if anybody was even home at the Ashcroft's house. This was eons before cell phones. The Ashcroft family lived on Warner Hill Road, in an area that was wooded and quite remote. That crank and flywheel with ring-gear darn well could have killed me.

There is more to the story. Murphy was a tough guy, obviously Irish, who liked to drink. A few months later, he died in a violent head-on collision. He was driving a 1947 Studebaker. At about 4 a.m. and while drunk, he turned to go into an all-night eatery, the Devon Diner, near the Housatonic River's Washington Bridge going over to Stratford. Murphy had crossed into the oncoming traffic heading east coming across the bridge. The highway was US Route #1 which runs from Maine to Florida. In that area of New England, it was commonly called the Boston Post Road.

Interstate highways didn't then exist. Trucks ran at night along the Boston Post Road. Also, most traffic lights at late night were ignored by the truckers in order to make time. Often the cities and towns along the way switched over the traffic lights to the caution or blinking mode, as opposed to red and green. My point is that late nighttime truck traffic on the Boston Post Road was heavy and fast. Drivers were in a hurry to deliver loads before the coming of daylight.

As Murphy crossed the lanes turning left, his Studebaker was struck head-on by an oncoming truck. That frontal impact drove the Studebaker's steering column into Murphy's chest. Before the days of modern steering wheels, safety and impact-absorbing designs didn't exist. In addition, cars of that vintage didn't have safety design features like seat belts and deployable air bags. The two studs supporting the steering wheel broke off and the steering column penetrated into Murphy's chest. Then Murphy's Studebaker was hit on its side by a second truck. That second hit caused the steering post, now with its two broken off studs, to violently spin about embedded within Murphy's chest cavity. I can recall later going with some friends to see Murphy's wrecked Studebaker. His pinkish lung tissue residue was still visible on the car's headliner.

The Dodge engine from Murphy never amounted to anything. Murphy was precisely correct in saying no knocks, no cracks, and won't burn oil. Its bits and pieces are now just a memory. My $25 vanished. One side benefit was that I had gained the experience of dismantling an entire engine down to every last piece. In the process I learned a considerable amount about automobile engines.

The Murphy junkyard engine story stands as an example of my stupidity, so the aftermath I felt needed to be told as well. Still to this day, I am aware of God's presence and how He has protected me. As that crankshaft and flywheel fell, I escaped serious injury and possibly even death by mere inches. Thanks again go to Herman.

The Twenty-Eight Miracles

AT TIMES IN MY LIFE, although not recently, I have told others about some of the supernatural happenings that have occurred in my lifetime. My listeners become spellbound. Many were to the point of being entertained. My listeners, often students in my classes, were typically on the edges of their chairs, straining to hear each word. What typically happened was that I was asked, when done, to tell yet another story. I call this scenario the Twenty-Eight Miracles. If I tell about 28 miracles, those listening will ask for yet one more, hence what I call the N+1 request. They were asking for N+1 when N was any finite number.

Jesus was asked to perform a miracle so that they could believe. The answer that Jesus gave was that the prophets had already stated many prophecies. In addition, all of those prophecies had been fulfilled with the coming of Christ. The Old Testament recorded over 400 prophecies. All were fulfilled with Christ's coming, death on the cross, and ascension into Heaven. If Christ performed one additional miracle, the +1 miracle would not change anything. Instead they would merely ask for yet another +1 miracle.

I take great comfort in the realization that the Old Testament prophets made 400+ prophecies regarding Christ and His coming. They will hang him on a tree. Not a single bone will be broken. They will cast lots for his garment. He will be of the house and lineage of David.

The Book of Isaiah was written about 700 years prior to the coming of Christ, and yet it is filled with prophecies that all have been fulfilled. If that is not enough to satisfy the doubter or skeptic, I doubt if the telling of my +1 miracle story would change their minds. The passages in Matthew 12: 38-42 and Matthew 16: 1-4 address the matter of persons asking that another miracle be performed. Jesus rebuked them. He is not a clown who performs miracles at the mere request of skeptics.

I will now return to tell more Dumb Dickie stories.

Yet Another Car Story – The Broken Stud

IN MY SENIOR YEAR of high school, I became more adept at working with engines. I had purchased a 1946 Ford coupe for $75 from George Spooner, a guy I will discuss later. As a part of the 1950s hot rod culture, I became fixated on the quest for more power under the hood. I decided to install a set of high compression heads. I bought some used aluminum racing heads, which is another mistake I won't go into.

The above photograph, taken from the Internet, shows a typical Ford V-8 flathead engine. These engines, with some variations, were used in Ford and Mercury cars from 1932 to

1953. Each flathead engine had two heads. In order to remove the heads, I had to loosen and remove the nuts on the studs. Each head was held on by 24 studs, each with a corresponding nut.

Wanting to install the new racing heads, I proceeded to remove the old factory installed cast iron heads. At this time the engine's stud nuts had been in place since the engine and car had been manufactured in 1946, hence over ten years. Obviously, rust had made removal difficult. The idea of using penetrating oil never dawned on me.

The above photograph, also from the Internet, shows a typical Ford V-8 engine with its heads removed. Please note the studs that protrude upward from the face of the block. In the assembly photograph above, some of the studs have not yet been installed. In my situation, the stud between the 3rd and 4th cylinders was the one that caused me problems. Ford numbered its cylinders 1-2-3-4 on the left side as shown, starting from the right or front of the engine. Ford provided a diagram with a specific sequence of tightening to follow when a head was reinstalled, starting with the centermost stud.

1946-48 V8 (24 Stud)

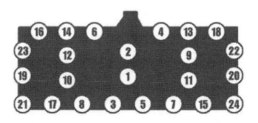

As per the above tightening sequence diagram, the stud that gave me grief was #10.

I proceeded to use my socket set and breaker bar applied to each stud nut in succession. Upon applying a large torque to one nut, I heard a sickening snap. The stud, #10, sheared off flush with the face of the block. Now I had to deal with a stud embedded in the engine's cast iron block.

I was working at Racine's Sunoco Service at the time. Another employee was the aforementioned George Spooner, a full-time mechanic at a local car dealership who had taken on an evening and weekend job for extra money. George pumped gas along with me at Racine's.

I looked up to George and respected his mechanical abilities. In addition, he drove a really cool car, a dazzling 1956 Crown Victoria Ford two-door hardtop. From my perspective, George had it all going for him.

I asked George for advice about my broken stud. My then-disabled car was parked at home in the driveway, so George never actually looked at it. He told me to drill a hole in the stud and get it out using a screw extractor.

Shown above is a commercially available set of screw extractors, commonly referred to as Easyouts®. Each tool is tapered so it can enter into a drilled hole in the broken screw or stud. Each extractor tool has a reverse twist. Then by turning it, assuming all goes well, one can extract the broken screw or stud.

I followed George's directions, but the screw extractor broke off. The broken-off stud was far too rusted and stuck to be removed easily. Now my broken stud problem had gotten decidedly worse. The screw extractor was made of hardened steel. The embedded broken part made it virtually impossible to drill the broken stud out or even attempt to drill the Easyout® remains.

I went back to George and told him the bad news. He told me to use a steel chisel and machinist's hammer. The idea was to crack the hardened steel out, as very hard steel also has the property of being brittle. George was saying, in effect, that by impacting the hardened steel, it would fracture. Once fractured, the screw extractor could be removed in bits.

I did as George instructed. But in repeatedly striking the broken screw extractor, I then cracked the engine block. The engine was completely ruined at that point.

Because the engine was now destroyed, I removed it. In the above photograph the defunct engine is on the ground to the left. I was dressed for going to U.S. Army Reserve summer camp in Camp Drum in upstate New York.

People tend to not believe me, but for that engine removal I timed myself to see how long it would take me. From when I first opened up my tool box until I closed my tool box, the entire time to remove that engine was 20 minutes. I had removed the engine on previous occasions, so I knew precisely what tools were needed, the necessary steps, and how to proceed. The car had been nosed into the garage to the left. I used a set of beams above the garage door to hook my chain hoist on. Careful examination of the engine in the above photograph shows that the head had already been removed and the exposed cylinders are visible.

Looking back, the lesson is that bad things like broken studs can happen and often will happen. In the Bonus Material section at the close of this book, I provide more detail. There I discuss the various options that skilled machinists have available to approach the broken stud removal task.

In hindsight my father, Albert Klein, could have solved the problem and saved my engine. At the time I was so distant from him that the idea of asking him for help never entered my mind. Also, at the time I lacked a true understanding of what machinists are capable of doing.

Back in those days I admired and even held up George Spooner as an idol because he was a certified professional mechanic. At that point, it was my life's ambition to become one. For schooling George had graduated from a trade school in Bridgeport, Connecticut, called Bullard-Havens Technical High School.

Much later in my life I came to recognize the vast differences between mechanics and machinists. The mechanic works with existing parts using existing tools. In stark contrast, a machinist will create any part as might be required. In addition, and of great importance, the machinist will make a tool if a special tool is required to do the job. This reminds me of Pop's often stated adage, "If you don't have the right tool, you're stuck."

As a sequel to the broken stud story, I bought a replacement engine from a local junkyard, but not Murphy's. The price was

$40. Back then, $40 was about equal to a week's wages for me. Buying that engine was a poor decision. Engines in cars in junkyards aren't there because they are in top working order. That junkyard engine developed a severe connecting rod knock as I drove out west to Grand View College in September of 1957. That was only a month or so after I had installed it.

Looking in the Rear-View Mirror

IN BOTH OF MY HIGH SCHOOL era automobile engine stories described above, I attempted to mess with perfectly good engines. The engines in both my 1936 Plymouth and the 1946 Ford were in top working order before I started tinkering with them. What I lacked at the time was somebody older and wiser to mentor me. I can't even think about all the wasted opportunities I didn't even recognize.

As for the used high compression racing heads, they ended up being a disaster. They never worked, and I eventually lost track of them. In this entire broken stud episode, it wasn't so much that I made a mistake or did something dumb. I tended to compound mistake after mistake. The amateur who thinks he/she can beat a professional ends up being the fool.

For my last two years of high school, I worked at Racine's Sunoco Service on Barnum Avenue. Along with the job came money. A mistake of some magnitude in my early life was to steadily earn money but to fail to understand why one should earn money. There was no discernable plan in place other than to feed my stomach with food I didn't need and to otherwise squander my earnings.

Now Comes a Colossal Blunder and Act of Stupidity

I CONSIDER MY DECISION to study and pursue mechanical engineering a serious blunder. I was clueless about what I was getting into.

I made the decision on my own when I was a senior in high school. By odd circumstances, I didn't enter the army as planned, but instead went to a small church-related school in Des Moines, Iowa.

As a disclaimer, choosing to be a mechanical engineer was a mistake for *me*—not a mistake in the larger sense for others.

In general, my values are incompatible with the mechanical engineering profession. Employers hire mechanical engineers for one specific purpose—to make a profit. My traits are focused on altruism and perfection. While I consider myself a highly skilled designer of mechanical things, I am so skilled that what I design stands above the marketplace. I tend to overdesign as I seek perfection. My inability to accept a shoddy design renders me an economic liability to the average company.

As the years went on, I was able to switch my focus and became an applied mathematician. Mathematics is based on absolute truths, embodied in things called theorems. That explains in part my decision to be a professor focused on systems theoretic principles as I could focus on perfection in design and place economic justification somewhere at the back of the line.

To repeat, I made the decision to study mechanical engineering while in high school. Nobody counseled me. I sought no counsel. My parents and immediate family didn't offer counsel. As a blue-collar working-class family, they were largely clueless about guiding me in my choices. My high school yearbook, Stratford High, Class of '57, succinctly sums up my affinity for things mechanical—*two loves: cars and guns.* Both are physical and mechanical.

With little thought, I just decided to pursue mechanical engineering. Only one person ever told me flat-out that I was making a mistake. That person was Fred Wilcoxson. Wilcoxson was the Assistant Fire Chief in Stratford and the father of my close friend Harry "Sputter" Wilcoxson. Fred Wilcoxson was blunt and caustic in his statements. He merely said it the way it was: mechanical engineering is a dead-end with little future, whereas electrical engineering was the better way to go. Being thick-headed, I brushed aside Wilcoxson's abrupt remark.

That was my error.

COLLEGE YEARS

Life Lessons 101
(1958-1965)

The Lost Years

LIKE MANY YOUNG MEN before and after me, I went through some dark times. At age 19, I made a grave mistake. I invited a college buddy to travel back east and stay at my parents' home. It was Christmas break, December 1958. I was in my second year of college, attending Grand View College in Des Moines, Iowa.

My friend was from Eastern Europe. He and his mother immigrated to the U.S. following WWII. Ivan was not familiar with American culture. He was a heavy smoker. After several days, my father erupted in anger at Ivan. The outburst was so ugly that my friend was no longer welcome in my father's home. Because I had invited Ivan there and he had traveled in my car, when he was ousted I felt ousted as well. For that reason, I stayed in Iowa for several years. Instead of returning home for the summer of 1959, I took on a job.

While in Iowa, I associated with some pretty dark guys. I could tell many stories about my life from 1959 until the summer of 1962, but most of those stories will have to wait.

For the summer of 1959, I ended up working for a guy 10 years my senior, known as Petie. My primary job working for Petie was to keep his racing stock car repaired and running. The race car's engine saw heavy duty. Parts wore out fast. We replaced the piston rings and rod-bearings every other week.

The engine was torn down and reassembled frequently. I was paid a dollar an hour, slept in Petie's shop building on a ratty sofa, and generally could have ample beer. An old refrigerator in the shop had cold beer. The shop building had been a small bank that went bust in the mid-1920s farm depression.

Petie's shop was located in the small rural and economically depressed town of Luther, Iowa. Petie was mostly of Scandinavian/Norwegian ancestry. Physically, he resembled a later U.S. President, Slick Willie, with his blond hair, blue eyes, medium height, big smile, and roundish-shaped face. And he resembled Clinton morally as well.

Petie was a lover, one who wasn't fussy about age. Sixteen and sixty were all the same to him. About sex, Petie described it saying, "It's all good. There is no bad." Petie once fathered a child with an unwed girl. That meant sending the girl to some rural home where she would stay during her pregnancy and delivery. Petie, being the caring and compassionate man he was, made the arrangements for the girl to give birth. After the baby was born, Petie then took and sold his own child for $500 plus medical expenses incurred. When he sat later laughing in a bar in Boone, Iowa, he remarked, "If I could do that every day, I'd go into business."

It is hard to describe the lowness of a scoundrel of Petie's order.

Petie's birth name was Byron K. Petersen (1929-c.1983), but his commonly known name was simply Petie. I once went to Petie's parents' home. They lived in a farmhouse as renters. Life was not extravagant. The farmhouse was so dated that it lacked indoor plumbing. The kitchen sink's water came from a handpump that drew water from a shallow well or possibly a rain-barrel cistern.

While there, Petie's mother explained that when she birthed Petie, it was a long and hard labor. She came close to dying. She then confided to me, "I wish that both Byron and I had died."

Petie had brought so much shame, pain, and disgrace to his parents and family.

In his high school days, Petie worked on cars. A friend known by the nickname "Squirrel" had a Ford Model A that wasn't running well. Squirrel's car engine would start but within a minute or two it would die. Squirrel went to Petie for some help. Petie told him the engine needed a tune-up. This involved new spark plugs, points, condenser, and timing check. That didn't help the problem. Next, Petie recommended doing a valve job. Together they did the valve job on Squirrel's four-cylinder engine. But alas, upon starting it up, the same thing happened. The engine stalled after a minute or so.

Petie then said that the engine needed to be rebuilt. They did that. But that didn't fix the problem either. Petie said the engine was no good, so they put in another engine. Again, the engine would run only a short time and then soon die.

It turned out that Petie had initially jammed three potatoes up the exhaust pipe of Squirrel's Model A. There are many lessons and morals to this story, but one thing was certain: Petie was a first-class jokester.

A second Squirrel-Petie story comes to mind, one that Squirrel told me himself. Squirrel attended high school in the town of Madrid, which was south of Luther. Squirrel drove his Model A between Luther and Madrid, a distance of about six miles, and would sometimes give Petie a ride. During one of these trips, Squirrel's Model A started to run poorly. It would run fine for a while, but then the engine would die. Squirrel and Petie would get out, open the hood, and try to diagnose the problem. At times the engine would start again. Off they would go, perhaps a quarter of a mile, perhaps 200 feet. Then they were once again looking at the engine trying to solve the problem. Squirrel would get frustrated to the point that he would start walking home, walking along the highway. Of course, Petie would suggest they try starting it just one more time.

Squirrel told me that his Model A always ran fine—except when Petie was riding along. After a year or so of all this foolery, Squirrel identified the problem. The gas tank on the Ford Model A was mounted ahead of the windshield as part of the cowl. The Model A had no fuel pump as it didn't need one—gas flowed to the carburetor by gravity.

The Model A also had a shut-off valve or petcock on the gas line going to the carburetor. That shut-off valve was mounted on the firewall under the dashboard. When Petie was riding in the passenger's seat he could use his toe to switch the fuel valve from on to off and back again at his whim. Squirrel joked about this many years later, as he told the story to me and others with a smile.

We raced Petie's superstock racecar weekly each racing season. We usually competed at the Knoxville, Iowa, one-half mile dirt track. Petie's car was #04. It was originally built using the frame and parts from a 1928 Ford Model T, but had a supercharged Ford Thunderbird V-8 engine. There was no clutch or transmission, just a disconnect box. There was no starter; it was started in gear by being pushed by a tow truck. The race track had several tow trucks to haul away racecars that wrecked or rolled over.

Petie worked at the John Deere plant in Ankeny, Iowa as a machinist. He was paid what was called piece-work. He also worked the graveyard shift. For many years he ran a horizontal turret lathe, turning out the same part. As a clever machinist, Petie devised his own tooling so that he could turn out his quota of parts in just a few hours. Petie's system was simple. After working a few hours, he would go to sleep in a storage cabinet on a pile of soft shop rags. If the foreman came by inquiring as to Petie's whereabouts, a co-worker told the foreman that Petie was in the bathroom. The foreman would walk to the bathroom to check. Meanwhile Petie's friend would rouse Petie from his sleep. Petie was back on the job before the foreman returned.

This was Petie's way of living. He slept at work while earning top wages.

As happens in factories, when a worker consistently gets paid more than standard because of piece-work high productivity, the company sends some green college kid, typically an industrial engineer, to retime the job. The green kid with his stopwatch, slide-rule, charts, and Taylor's metal-cutting equation was no match for Petie. The kid observed Petie at his turret-lathe producing parts the standard way. When the kid was momentarily distracted, Petie used an elbow to jam the cutting tool. Finally, the college graduate took over the lathe to do the work himself. Petie's trick was that he had switched cutting fluids. The tool bits tore up, slowing the work.

At one point, Petie was faced with an aggressive young engineer attempting to retime the job. One of Petie's friends took a cup of fine grinding compound. This grinding compound was normally used at John Deere suspended in oil for precise grinding of bearing finishes. Recall, this was all happening during the night shift, as Petie worked nights for the extra bonus. The outside parking lot was dark. Petie's friend opened the young engineer's car hood and poured the fine cutting powder into the car's crankcase. Within a week's time, the engine was totally worn out—destroyed by no obvious cause. The engineer had to replace his car's engine. He still persisted in trying to retime the job. But alas, after another week went by his new engine soon became junk. The replacement engine suffered a similar fate as the first engine. The message was clear—or should have been—forget about retiming Petie's lathe operation.

Young engineering graduates are not trained to understand the risks of messing with shop employees like Petie. These shop guys were both resourceful and cunning. I learned much about life during my dark years. I also understood the evilness and total absence of morals associated with the likes of Petie.

Petie mostly took advantage of vulnerable females. He never

went after attached females. Instead he went for younger single women, an occasional divorcee, and even widows.

I recall Petie getting a black eye one time when a new guy started dating the woman he'd been seeing. Now, Petie didn't challenge other men for women. He once explained to me, "I'm a lover, not a fighter." In the case of the black eye incident, Petie's response was low. He still had a key to the woman's apartment. While the woman was out, Petie snuck back into the apartment. After gathering his belongings, Petie did one more thing. He punctured small holes in the woman's birth control diaphragm. The woman conceived a child, fathered by the new lover. Petie had a good laugh over that.

Des Moines was known as the Hartford of the West because of the many insurance companies located there. Insurance companies attract and hire secretarial staff. Girls from rural towns and farms would come to Des Moines for employment. They would rent or share a room or modest apartment. Petie had an amazing ability to hook up with such girls, usually by moving in with them and becoming a bed partner, among other things. When Petie moved in, he hung some shirts in a closet, put some socks and underwear in a drawer, and put his shoes under the bed. He could carry all his stuff on the seat of his car. Petie slept with them, ate food from the refrigerator, and availed himself of whatever he fancied. The word "gigolo" comes close to being an apt descriptor for Petie. When I worked for Petie in the shop, he would just say, "I need to go to town," implying Des Moines. He would be gone several days, obviously getting in some loving. Whenever a girl fell out of favor, there were many more waiting. Petie was a handsome guy with an infectious smile and a sharp Thunderbird to boot. Attracting females was never a problem for Petie.

Petie had two fancy new Ford Thunderbirds. The first was a 1957. One night while obviously intoxicated, Petie rolled it over on a desolate road. He had a car loan as the Thunderbird was close to new. The loan required Petie to carry insurance for the car's collision replacement. Petie didn't want to fight with an insurance company only to end up driving a repaired Thunderbird. Since the automobile had flipped over, some gasoline was dripping out of the gas fill cap. Petie lit a match, then threw it onto the gas—and watched as a virtually new Thunderbird was destroyed beyond repair by fire. Later, he bought the burned-out Thunderbird from the insurance company. That engine ended up in the #04 superstock race car.

Petie's next car was a 1959 Thunderbird. Petie and one of his more affluent bed partners drove it to Tijuana, Mexico. There Petie had it painted in candy-apple red hand-rubbed lacquer. This required multiple paint applications and much labor, of low cost south of the border. Of course, Petie's current lovemate paid all the expenses for the trip.

The Volkswagen Beetle was just appearing in America. Gas mileage was astonishing in terms of miles per gallon, at least as compared to most American cars. One of Petie's friends had a VW Beetle, and constantly boasted about his fuel economy. The more the friend boasted, the higher went his claimed miles per gallon. At times he was getting between 50 and 75 miles per gallon.

All this came to an end and the boasting stopped when Petie's prank was discovered. Petie, being a jokester, had been adding extra gasoline into the VW's tank. Few remember this now, but early VW Beetles didn't have a gas gauge. The VW had a reserve feature so that upon running out of gas, you could switch to reserve and get additional miles and thus make it to a station for fuel. The friend never noticed Petie's added gas contributions as the VW had no fuel gauge, so he believed he was getting incredible mileage.

Because he was blond and handsome, some women sought to have a baby by Petie. Once when he was in the army stationed in Cuba, a Cuban prostitute said to him during intercourse,

"You give me blonde bambino." Petie replied, "Yeah Honey, I'm trying."

During that time in Luther, Iowa, one of my cars was a 1935 Ford roadster. I was once driving it to the Greater Des Moines Drag Race. My problem was that the floorboards were rusted and had some holes. Engine fumes made for uncomfortable breathing, as I was getting gassed out. The roadster was open since the original canvas retractable top had long before disintegrated. I was running late for the race check-in, so time was critical. While driving, I did a bad thing—I loosened the two wingnut knobs that held the windshield in place. On a roadster the windshield could be opened for increased frontal air. Then I pushed the bottom of the windshield forward several inches. Before I could tighten the two knobs, the windshield violently flipped up and backwards. I was traveling about 60 MPH. The windshield cracked me on the skull. I started to bleed profusely, as most head wounds are accompanied by much bleeding.

This story of how a roadster's front windshield flipped and struck me on the head established one point. Oncoming wind can unfurl a windshield, a sail, or similar appendage. This attribute of a sail to unfurl itself reappears in a companion Dumb Dickie authored book, *The Deadly Gamble: A Post-Morten of the World Trade Center Collapse* (2019). I later employed these designs in my research into stabilization of tall buildings. The many other stories about my life as a stock car race mechanic working for a scoundrel will be set in reserve for some future writing endeavor. Rest assured, I never have to struggle to come up with topics and stories to write about.

For years during my professorship at the University of Illinois, I pondered if the day would come when one of Petie's many flower children would show up in a class. That never happened, but a U.S. President did show up. Slick Willie was a spitting image of Petie, both physically and in moral character. History states that William Jefferson Blythe Jr. fathered Bill, but I still find the resemblance to be uncanny.

In those days of visiting Petie in Luther, Iowa, I was at a point in life where my worldly possessions were few. Most of what I had would easily fit into the back seat and trunk of a car. I didn't own a camera. I have no photographs to show what Petie looked like. I'm sure the typical reader is wondering how I fit into life in Luther, and did I partake? I was content to just work on cars, the racecar in particular. I slept in the shop on an old sofa, as stated. I was aware of Petie's lifestyle and affinity for women. Petie only rarely brought any lady friends to the shop. He lived in a dual world, a world composed of two distinct spheres that did not co-mingle. I saw only the shop sphere. I had zero interest in Petie's taste in women.

In my senior year of high school, I became entrapped by a sophomore girl, Emily. That entrapment made me hesitant to get trapped a second time—at least until I decided it was time. During my two years attending Grand View College in Des Moines, 1957-1959, I never dated a single Grand View girl. I tended to enjoy working on cars, being unencumbered, and drinking a few beers.

On several occasions I even pulled an engine behind the main dormitory building. I used a chain hoist hooked to a heavy overhanging tree limb. At one point, a girl came up to me asking what I was doing. She said I should sell my three old cars and buy one good car. Then she added in an obviously frustrated tone, "Just what do I have to do to get your attention?"

I had been so immersed in cars that dating her never entered my mind. I had previously sized her up as spoiled, demanding, and self-centered. I will also add that God had endowed her with an impressive body. She was exactly the type of female I was determined to avoid.

The last time I saw Petie was in the spring of 1962. He was in bed, but still maintained his optimistic and smiling self. He was in bed because he'd been in a bar fight. A bartender had gotten a shotgun out to settle a rowdy situation. One of Petie's companions was a hothead who provoked the bartender. When the shotgun was pointed at Petie, he grabbed for the barrel end to swing it down and away. The shotgun discharged, hitting him in the kneecap. This altercation took place in Lineville, Missouri. Petie and two other guys were driving to Kansas City to buy some racecar stuff. As alcoholics, they couldn't pass a bar without stopping for a drink. Petie and his two companions were strangers there. After the altercation, the locals tossed Petie and his friends out onto the street. By the time the sheriff was called, the locals all had the story decided that Petie had somehow shot himself.

As I left Luther, Iowa, I retrieved my few personal belongings from the shop, mostly tools. I never saw Petie again. He died in his early fifties of alcoholism.

It is timely to terminate Petie stories and return to Dickie stories.

My Life in Iowa, a Roast Pig

I NEED TO EXPLAIN how I handled my military obligation during the lost years. I spent five years mostly in Iowa, from September 1957 until June 1962. During that time, I was obligated to attend U.S. Army enlisted reserve meetings and two-week summer camps. In all, I was a reservist for slightly over seven years. I served with Korean War veterans, but was honorably discharged before the Vietnam War era. I wasn't drafted for Vietnam as I had already served my 7 years by the time the war started, since I had originally enlisted in the reserves while in high school at age 17.

As an active reservist, whenever I moved to a new location, such as the Iowa City area, I transferred to a local reserve unit. I was in the Iowa City reserve unit until sometime in 1962.

While not of my choosing, I was assigned to be a cook. As a cook, I became familiar with serving large groups, in excess of a hundred men. I was living with college friends, mostly associated with Acacia Fraternity, at the time.

In the spring of 1961, I embarked on a great project—to put on a pig roast. I asked questions of some Amish guys in the army outfit. One of them had roasted a whole hog, so I got some basics from him. Of course, I already knew all about how to roast a pig, having seen enough Hollywood Robinson Crusoe types roasting pigs. I wasn't interested in digging a deep hole for a Hawaiian luau, as I was going to a public park. Instead, my decision was to roast the pig on a spit over charcoal.

The first thing one needs is the pig. I decided on a live-weight of about 90 pounds. That weight was determined by the number of guests and taking into account the losses for hide, hoofs, internal organs, back-fat, and bone. A pig will yield half of its weight in edible meat. I drove with friends to a fraternity buddy's farm close by. We caught our pig. We put the pig live into a burlap sack and then put the pig on the backseat floor of my car. At the butcher shop, we discovered the pig had gained weight. The 90-pound pig somehow now weighed in at 135 pounds.

The day for the pig roast came. A few friends and I got the pig, 80 pounds of charcoal, and all the anticipated equipment and supplies. We dug a shallow pit, lit the charcoal, and placed the pig on a long steel pipe as our spit. I used two car bumper jacks to support the spit, one jack on each end. Of course, we had a crank attached to the pipe, just like it is done in the movies. Cranking a pig over an open fire for eight hours required the consumption of adequate beer.

A problem arose when the temperature probes inserted into the pig never exceeded 135 degrees F. That is bad. Fresh pork needs a greater temperature to kill what is called *trichinella spiralis.* The guests started arriving. As I recall, I had invited about 40 or 50 people. Someone was hastily sent to town to buy more charcoal. As the pig finally started to warm (after much charcoal had been added), two other problems arose: the pig started to fall apart, and the spit turned but the pig just hung in the same position and didn't follow the turning of the spit. I had cross skewers through the pig and steel spit, but nothing kept the skewers from falling out once the pig cooked, giving off fat and drippings.

Given this myriad of problems, about the best you can do is

to hope that the guests get drunk and don't notice the under-cooked pink pork. A second option would be to send someone to town for hamburgers and franks. I made it through the day, but it was pretty dumb of me to believe Hollywood as opposed to doing my homework. The one thing I learned that day was how *not* to roast a pig.

Road Rage in Reverse

DURING MY YEARS living in Iowa, I was an on-and-off student. At times I attended the University of Iowa. When not in school, I twice held down jobs working at Collins Radio Company in Cedar Rapids. At the University of Iowa, I joined Acacia Fraternity.

In May of 1962, I drove with two fraternity friends, Bill and Bob, to Bloomington, Indiana for a weekend. We stayed at the Acacia Fraternity house on the Indiana University campus. On Sunday morning, the three of us got back into my car to start our drive back to Iowa City, a drive of possibly six hours. We were in my sharp-looking white '55 Chevrolet convertible. As it was a warm sunny day, the convertible's top was down. I was driving. The two other guys were seated with me, three across, on the front seat. Convertibles are fun, but sitting in the back seat is uncomfortable as it is too windy at highway speeds. This was before interstates, so we made the trip on two-lane state highways. As we passed through each town, speed limits were in place. We drove slower in towns.

We had driven north through Indiana on a good highway that took us to U.S. Route 150 headed west. We came to the small town of Veedersburg, Indiana.

As we traveled through Veedersburg at a gentle speed, we

encountered a problem. A car came up behind me, within a few feet of my rear bumper. I didn't notice the car in my rearview mirror until I heard its engine revved-up and racing. Clearly, the driver was itching for some type of confrontation, or at least scaring the wits out of my two buddies and me. Because we were in a top-down convertible, the three of us were plainly visible. Both Bill and Bob were slender and tall. They both were clean-cut and had short crew-cut hairstyles. I won't speak for myself, but my two buddies were archetypal college kids, nowhere near looking like seasoned street fighters.

Obviously, the aggressive driver and his buddies were belligerents trying to provoke a confrontation. They just couldn't resist the temptation to have some fun with three wimpy-looking college guys riding in a top-down convertible.

My first reaction was to do a brake check, which means that I slightly tapped my brake pedal. This flashed my brake lights, sending a signal that I had seen the threatening car—and to back off. But the car behind me again came up close. Again the engine raced.

With no other warning, I made my defensive move. I slammed on my brakes. The car behind me ran into my rear bumper. In such a scenario, several things are certain.

First, my rear bumper goes up upon the strong application of my brakes.

Next, the vehicle behind me does a nose-dive of sorts.

This combination causes my rear bumper to impact the other car's grill and radiator. In this case, the car behind me was totaled, as it wasn't a new car and had little value. Its engine thrust forward, causing the fan to destroy the radiator. The car's front end was destroyed, as the front wheels were now pigeon-toed.

And lastly, the guy in the rear is always at fault.

We were on an Indiana state highway, so an Indiana state trooper came. The other car had three tough guys. There was much shouting and posturing. They had been drinking. A witness told the trooper that the rear guys had thrown out empty beer cans.

The trooper asked me what happened. I said, "I braked because a cat ran in front of my car." The witness, an older guy who'd been out mowing his lawn, remarked to the trooper, "Yes, I remember seeing a cat around here."

The aggressor had a suspended driver's license. The state trooper took him away in handcuffs. The aggressor's car was totaled. Coolant was running over the highway and its front end was whipped out. It was not drivable.

My '55 Chevy was hurt slightly, but quite drivable. My buddy, Bill Nissen, was totally caught off guard. "Trooper, what are you doing?" Bill asked me.

My nickname in those days was "Trooper." I was dubbed that name because of a common phrase I used, "Let's get the troops out of the hot sun." I coined that phrase to express my frustration with Army Reserve officers having the troops stand in the hot sun. Anybody with half a brain would know it is better to stand in the shade.

My point in recounting this story is clear. I can be nice and polite, but when threatened, I will turn and use every weapon at my disposal, including my car. I am like a rattlesnake. I will give a warning, but when my warning is not heeded, I strike.

Mario Puzo's book, *The Godfather*, is filled with admonitions. Don Vito Corleone says some people go around shouting, "kill me, kill me." A day may come when somebody will oblige them. The three guys in Veedersburg were shouting out, "kill me, kill me." I was kind to them. Veedersburg certainly became a better place. Those guys were less inclined to repeat that stunt. Perhaps they even learned to respect others. I never bothered to seek remedy for the damage to my car. I had bigger fish to fry.

Getting My Life Back on Track

IN JUNE 1962, I departed from Iowa and returned to my parents' home in Connecticut. The gulf between my father and me had been forgotten, or at least set aside. That story aspect is complex and personal. In brief, I had written a letter to my father following my ouster in 1958. In that letter I stated my side of the breach. Unknown to me until several decades later, my letter never reached my father. Instead, it was first opened by my mother. She used forgery to amend my letter by switching out some of my harsher words. Upon returning home in 1962, nothing was said about the matter. I was happy with tranquility and didn't dig up old grievances.

June of 1962 coincided with my brother Donald's return from Germany with his young family. I soon moved with Don's family to Bellefonte, Pennsylvania. Don entered Penn State for his doctorate in microbiology. I applied to Penn State's undergraduate program to complete my degree in mechanical engineering. In June a year later, in 1963, I became engaged. Marjorie and I set a wedding date of September 1, 1963. To be closer to campus and to be able to study better, I moved for the summer of 1963 into a rooming house close to campus with other engineering students.

It was then and only then that I discovered a prior mistake in my life. By chance, I became a member of a study group. The guys in the rooming house had access to old course files and notably old exams. I did homework assignments sitting with fellow students. My grades as well as material comprehension were boosted. I was then 24 years old. I realized that I had never before learned how to study. That error of my upbringing had cost me dearly.

Upon getting married, over Labor Day weekend of 1963, I became more adept at focusing on school.

When Marjorie and I were married, we had just $13 between us. Fortunately, Marjorie had a job. She taught in the Tyrone, Pennsylvania grade school for $4,000 per year. We watched our money carefully, virtually to the penny. Our weekly food and shopping budget was $3. This included toothpaste, soap, and toilet paper. I recall once being in the grocery check-out. The total came to $3.12. We put something back.

A Hitchhiker's Guide

FROM TYRONE, PENNSYLVANIA, I commuted thirty miles each day to State College to attend classes. After driving a car for a few days, I sought a better solution. I tried hitchhiking.

Because of World War II, hitchhiking was accepted. During the war, the public was encouraged to give a serviceman a lift. Hitchhiking remained in our culture, at least up until the advent of the interstate highway system. I soon discovered that the secret for success was rooted in several things: be well dressed, display a small sign giving your desired destination, and pick a location where traffic has slowed. I found out that I could hitchhike from A to B faster than I could usually drive. In the right position, I often had a ride in one or two minutes. The drivers picking up hitchhikers were single men, often traveling salesmen. They tended to drive over the speed limit. I could go good distances, such as the 100 miles from Des Moines to Iowa City. Again, hitchhiking was fast, free, and convenient. Only rarely did I ever get stranded.

From Tyrone to State College, the same guys started picking me up. I finally decided to just car pool with them. Instead of me driving once each week, I gave the driver $1 each week. My cost to commute was 20 cents per day, both ways.

These Tyrone guys were locals who commuted to work on

construction in State College. I learned much from them and how they survived. I learned to spot deer, especially in the early dawn. Deer are there, but most people don't see them because they fail to look.

As poor people, poaching deer was a part of their culture. Like Robinhood, if they gave to the poor and established that reputation, no jury of poor people would ever convict them.

They would spotlight deer at night. The preferred rifle was a simple .22 rimfire. As a deer would freeze in a spotlight's glare, the men would shoot it through the eyeball. The deer would drop on the spot. It was quiet. Then, they would give a hind quarter to Widow Jones. The community understood that the deer were shot to allow these people to survive.

Our culture has changed. Hitchhiking is no longer effective. However, I do have some advice about hitching if necessary.

Purchase or borrow a gas can. Stand along a highway with your gas can. You will get a ride, often the first or second car.

If you are serious about hitchhiking, get a new red metal gas can. I am thinking of the jerry can 5-gallon type. Cut it open with a metal cutting saw. Install hinges and a latch. Recall, you are doing this to a new gas can, so the inside is clean. You then use the 5-gallon gas can as your suitcase. The driver picking you up will eventually wonder where your stranded car is. You explain the ruse. The driver will laugh and you will have made a new friend. When hitchhiking with your gas can, never stick out your thumb. You won't be arrested if you are just standing innocently along a highway. If a cop bothers you, you are there waiting for a friend.

Never be standing on an interstate. It's better to pick a location near an entrance. One slow car going by is worth a thousand passing you at highway speeds.

If you are serious about hitchhiking longer distances, go to the pilot's lounge at an airport. Pilots love flying. They love to share their love for flying. Approach them, be polite, and tell them that you would someday like to take flying lessons. Ask where they are going. You may be invited along. Keep a flight log to document your travels, and to show your good character.

The ultimate method to hitchhike is to be in distress and carrying a baby. In Boris Pasternak's *Dr. Zhivago*, the old woman running alongside the train has a baby. In the movie *Titanic*, the arch-villain grabs a crying child; he uses the child as a pretense to get in the ladies-only lifeboat.

The Metamorphosis of Dickie

I FEEL COMPELLED to inject a story about the afternoon of Christmas Eve 1963. The significance of the story isn't about being dumb, but rather it concerns a change that was taking place within me. As I reflect on my childhood and upbringing, I was the little brother. I lived in a family atmosphere where I was ridiculed, belittled, and put down. My way of dealing with that environment was to become phlegmatic. The word from the Greek implies a person filled with phlegm, and thus passive. Upon getting married and leaving my childhood environment, a different person emerged.

I was undergoing a metamorphosis. I started to become assertive and commanding. This was a gradual process, but the metamorphosis caused a new creature to burst forth. One pivotal incident in my life occurred on December 24, 1963. Marjorie and I had been married just under four months. We were spending our first Christmas holiday at her parents' farm in Iowa.

Marjorie and I had driven straight through from Pennsylvania to her parents' farm near Davenport. As we left Pennsylvania and drove west, the heater and defroster in our 1953 Ford sedan weren't up to the job. The outside temperatures dropped as we drove west. It was bitterly cold. By the time we crossed the Mississippi River into Davenport, it was about -30 degrees F outside. The defroster could barely keep up. I was driving and looking out of a small peep-hole the size of a softball. The rest of the windshield was frosted up. On top of all that, it was late at night and dark. I was wrapped in a sleeping bag while driving. Only my eyes and nose were not covered. Marjorie was wrapped up as well. The trip was grueling to say the least.

After we arrived at Marjorie's parents' home, a request was made for someone to go into Davenport for some last-minute shopping. Marjorie and I were given a list that required stops at several stores.

One stop was at a supermarket for the sole purpose of buying a frozen ham, then on sale. Marjorie's mother was known as a cherry-picker in supermarket terminology. She would purchase only the items on sale that are drastically reduced in price just to attract shoppers. These items are referred to in the trade as loss leaders. The idea, of course, is that once shoppers are in the door, they will buy other items that are not on sale. But not cherry-pickers.

Marjorie and I purchased the frozen ham. I didn't need a shopping cart just for one ham. As the ham was large, I carried it using both hands, akin to holding a basketball with two hands. I was carrying it within the usual brown paper sack. As I recall, the ham was approximately 20 pounds. I had a modest headache due to being tired and having driven through the night. In those days, the idea of stopping at a motel was unheard of for us. Our budget was too stretched for motels. We also never budgeted the time.

As we exited the supermarket, I was moving at a modest pace. I certainly wasn't running or even walking fast. Shoppers usually walk directly to their parked cars. Traffic may come along in front of the store entrance, but the area is where shoppers commonly walk in and out. Marjorie and I were perhaps 50 feet out the door on our way to our car.

The driver of an early 1950s Chevrolet objected to me walking where I was. I had not taken notice of the car. I'm sure it was not there when I stepped out onto the traffic area. I was walking on what I believed to be a parking lot, an area safe for walking. The first indication I had of the car was the sound of its horn blaring. I had been moving diagonally away from the storefront, and my back was to the car.

Upon hearing the horn, instead of jumping or running, I froze. I stopped in my tracks. As the blaring continued, I turned. At the same instant that I turned, the driver suddenly accelerated the car—directly at me. All this happened in a split second. It was near dusk and the overhead parking lot lights created a glare on the car's windshield. I saw only the glare. I had no ability to see the occupants or the driver. The car stopped momentarily, its front bumper less than five feet from me. The horn continued to sound. Then the driver hit the accelerator to the floorboard. The car came right at me.

I was a pedestrian walking out of a store in the store's parking lot. Pedestrians have the right of way, certainly over motor vehicles. My body language was saying, "Who in the world do you think you are, buddy?"

As the vehicle lurched at me, I executed a fancy side-step. My side-step was similar to the side-step of a bullfighter, but with several differences:

I had no warning that a charging bull was about to come at me.

I lacked a red cape, but I did have a sizeable frozen ham in my hands.

The bull charging me was heavier than your average bull; it was mechanized and driven by a man who obviously had some mental disorder. Clearly, the driver was, at minimum, temporarily insane and taking out his outrage against me.

I pushed the ham away at arm's length, which caused my body to get out of the vehicle's path. I narrowly avoided being hit and run over. The car missed me by mere inches. As the car sped past me, my outstretched hands threw the ham downward into the car's front windshield. I was then on the passenger's side of the vehicle. The ham hit directly in front of the front passenger.

In sum, an irrational driver attempted to kill me. There was no question that the driver saw me, as he was at a stop and then blew his car horn. It wasn't just a tiny beep, but rather a long blast as he held down on the horn. He had deliberately attempted to run me over. This was no accident but rather a deliberate attack—with the objective of running me over. If I had not quickly side-stepped, I am certain the outcome would have been fatal. To my knowledge, this was the only time an attacker had tried to kill me. I had been in fights before, but not confrontations that included attempted manslaughter. I call it manslaughter because I believe that no jury would accept that premeditation existed. The driver didn't plan my death, but rather something drove him over the brink in a non-premeditated reaction or stressful moment. I am not an attorney, so I may be confused about the role of premeditation. I also lack an understanding of the distinction between such things as negligent homicide, manslaughter, murder-II, and murder-I. I trust and pray that I don't ever need to know.

The driver was a man, possibly fifty or maybe older. He had two grown men riding with him, possibly his sons. An infant was also on board. After the ham smashed the windshield, the driver hit the brakes. All three men suddenly got out of the car. I was on the verge of being drawn into a fight. All this time my bride Marjorie was beside me, totally surprised.

Fists did not fly, although the two sons postured as if ready to fight. The older man, the driver, demanded that I pay him $25 for his windshield. I now want to comment on the presence of the infant. This incident happened long before infants and younger children were required to be in boosters or infant seats.

The baby had been in the lap of one of the men sitting in the front passenger's seat. The infant was directly in the line of the ham's impact. I said nothing at the time about the infant's safety or well-being, recognizing that it was critical that I not admit or suggest fault. Marjorie was completely unprepared for this incident and the confrontation. She was near openly urging that I pay the man the $25.

At this point, as a trained street-wise fighter, I did two things.

First, I used voice projection aimed at all present. By using voice projection, I was able to establish that I was in charge. The arguing and posturing immediately stopped. I also had to get Marjorie quieted and not screaming that I should pay the man. Advice like that was the last thing I needed after an attempt on my life.

Using a loud voice, I said, "Marjorie, get out your lipstick. Now mark the placement of my feet on the pavement, and then the position of the vehicle's front tire."

Upon lunging the ham into the windshield, I had deliberately remained in place. My feet had not moved.

My next move was to refocus the event's setting. Because of my wits as applied to altercation control, I knew to turn a shouting match and potential fist fighting scenario into a litigation—a matter of law and evidence.

All shouting stopped. The man asked, "What are you doing with that lipstick?"

I replied, "I am gathering evidence."

My strategy was to both silence Marjorie and turn the incident into a legal matter.

Soon a Davenport policeman arrived. Cell phones didn't exist at that time, so I assume the store manager had made the call. The driver exclaimed to the cop, "This man smashed my windshield and I want him arrested!"

The cop turned to me.

At that point, I just wanted to go back with Marjorie to her parents' home. It was late afternoon or possibly after sunset. It was Christmas Eve. My statement to the cop was simple, "If he wants me charged, then I will file charges against him for trying to run me over."

I didn't explain that the driver had suddenly and deliberately accelerated his car at me so as to harm or even kill me. I had avoided being hurt. I had by then retrieved the ham from the windshield. Being frozen and in a brown shopping bag, it was perfectly fine. Filing charges would mean spending Christmas Eve at a police station and possibly being detained. Not to mention lawyers and return visits. Also, the cop could see the smashed windshield, but he hadn't seen me being assaulted. It was not in Marjorie's world understanding to say anything to corroborate what had transpired. I was alone and had vocal, irate people pointing fingers at me. Police are probably nice people, but it is delusionary to suggest that a cop can arrive at a commotion and put every detail into place. In my world view, cops are characteristically slow or even blind to seeing detail.

The cop decided on the spot that the matter was civil and not criminal. My threat to file counter-charges took the wind out of the driver's demands. The cop said that our respective attorneys could resolve the matter. The man and I exchanged names and addresses. I have no memory of the cop even taking our names or asking for witness statements.

In hindsight, I consider the cop's performance to be substandard. An obvious crime of attempted vehicular homicide was committed. I can assure you that in my world, I depend on myself long before I depend on police responding.

As the events unfolded, I instinctively recognized that one never pays for damages on the spot. Doing so constitutes an admission of guilt. A month or so later I received a letter from the man's attorney asking that I pay $75 for damages. I wrote a letter back explaining that his client had tried to harm me as a pedestrian, and that his client, the driver, opted to hit my flesh with iron. I never heard another word.

Upon returning to Marjorie's home on Christmas Eve, we said that we got all items, had a good time, and that Richard was involved in an altercation—and that Richard threw a ham through a car's windshield.

As a point of background, I once had a college roommate, Mike Walsh, who worked summers flagging traffic through construction zones. He had his flag on a stout stick. If cars came by too fast and too close, his response was to take out a headlamp with the stick. If the cars were excessively speeding, he would go for the windshield. Mike never had a car stop. In my case the ham did the trick.

I wish to acknowledge Frank Lesneski Sr., the father of a high school friend. Mr. Lesneski mentored me in varied aspects of street-fighting. I will defer telling the many things here that Lesneski taught me. He had been a semi-professional prize fighter in the 1930s. I owe much to Lesneski for my education and grounding in street-fighting.

Dickie Klein had shown his true grit. I can be a nice guy, but when provoked, I am capable of hitting back hard and with little warning. I'm sure that Marjorie thought she was marrying a docile guy. Yes, I am that but I am also an adept and experienced person with street situational awareness skills. I wish to remark to my faithful reader, do not associate the image of street-fighter with scum or filth. Instead think of polite, resourceful, vigilant, and prepared on a moment's notice. I had the benefit of being schooled by masters. There is no shame whatsoever associated with situational awareness and defensive reactions. When bad things happen, a whole new being kicks into place. It's that simple.

My Struggles with Differential Equations

DURING MY COLLEGE YEARS, I attended four different colleges and universities: Grand View College in Des Moines, Iowa; the University of Iowa in Iowa City; Pennsylvania State University in University Park, Pennsylvania; and lastly Purdue University in West Lafayette, Indiana. Because my story is interwoven with so many topics and timelines, I feel compelled to make an observation at this point. For each transition to a new school, my ability to gain admission to the next step was dubious at best. In virtually all cases, my most recent grades or the passing of a standardized national examination allowed me to make the next cutoff, although just barely.

I want to recount two stories related to making the often perilous cut to the next level. The first story concerns a course called Ordinary Differential Equations, sometimes referred to as DEQ. DEQ is the course you take after completing three semesters of calculus. Moreover, DEQ represents possibly the most dreaded course encountered by engineering students. For Dumb Dickie, that applied double or maybe triple. For me, that course was a brick wall that I had extreme difficulty getting past. I did so poorly—three times, in fact—that I dropped the course just before the cut-off for the drop date. On the fourth try, it became a matter of do or die. I was in a large section at Penn

State. By chance I happened to get a professor with the nickname Santa Claus, or so I found out later. His actual name was Professor Rodgers. He was nonchalant about the material, and I liked his style. He didn't lecture. Instead, during classes he had students get up and do the homework problems on the blackboard. There was no pressure. While at the blackboard, the students would comment on how they were solving the problem.

Many engineering classes are "crank-turners"—you can do the problems in a step-by-step fashion and crank out answers. DEQ was the epitome of a crank-turning class.

At the end of the semester, I recall Professor Rodgers instructing his graduate graders to give the students 70 percent A grades and 30 percent B grades. There were no grades given lower than B. No C's, D's, or F's. In his class, I was in the bottom 30 percent. I was most likely the anchor man, the student with the lowest point total. But that didn't matter. My grade was a B. I had passed DEQ! A miracle had happened in front of my eyes.

In those days, a C was considered an average grade. I received a B, which in most circles was outstanding. In the world of mathematics, most A grades were reserved for the math majors rather than engineers. I would have felt lucky just to pass that long-dreaded course with a D. Not only did I pass, that B from Santa Claus dramatically influenced my life's journey. Santa exists. He even gave Dumb Dickie the best present of all—a very respectable grade in DEQ, unquestionably the hardest course for engineering students.

My second story is related to the first. I completed my BS requirements in March 1964, as Penn State used the quarter system as opposed to semesters. My wife, Marjorie, had three months left on her teaching contract in Tyrone. I had applied to Penn State's Master of Science program starting in March 1964, but I was rejected. My undergraduate grades weren't worthy of my gaining admission to graduate school.

I wasn't too concerned as I had already decided to leave engineering and enter law school. I vaguely envisioned a future in patent law. Because of my high score on the LSAT (Law School Admission Test), I had been accepted into the University of Michigan law program starting the summer of 1964. I had applied to Michigan because it was rated as one of the top five law schools in the nation at the time.

Because I had one quarter free, I decided to take classes at Penn State in mechanical engineering as an unclassified (non-degree) student. Why not get a few graduate courses on my transcript before law school? It seemed like a great idea. Penn State had a provision whereby any graduate could take some classes after graduation as a non-degree candidate.

I paid my tuition and did the paperwork, but I needed an advisor to sign for my course selections. I was sent to Dr. Donald Olson, Associate Head of the Mechanical Engineering Department. He was surprised because he'd never had an unclassified student before.

"Why aren't you seeking a degree?" Olson asked.

"I applied but was denied admission," I explained.

"What grade did you get in DEQ?"

"B."

"Wait here," he said, rising from his desk chair. He left, then returned five minutes later with some papers in hand. "If anybody wants to go to school that bad, we won't stop him."

I told Marjorie that night that I was now admitted to Penn State as a degree program graduate student. The B from Professor Rodgers in DEQ got me into Penn State's graduate degree program. Without doubt, that grade changed the entire direction of my life.

The reader would be correct in sensing that I have strong opinions about how Differential Equations is taught, why it is taught, and what the world's problem-solvers need to know.

In order to understand how and why DEQ exists and is taught, it helps to understand the role of mathematics departments in the educational culture. The vast majority of students taking math courses are not math majors. Math is taught as a service to heathens such as engineering students, accountancy majors, biologists, and such. The math department provides courses for these brutes. Math professors disdain such teaching assignments, but the budget the math department receives is there only because of the service courses provided.

Math professors have little interest in doing a good job. The students are forced to take math courses. The math professors in turn dislike teaching service courses. Most schools have math majors, although few in comparison to other fields of study, so some higher level math courses are there for the holy ones: the math majors. Most math professors are relegated to teaching service courses, be it calculous, DEQ, or statistics, as only a few courses exist solely for math majors.

The topics covered in traditional DEQ courses haven't changed over the last century or two. The DEQ course serves as a filter—to weed out weak or unmotivated students. The engineering departments don't really care, as having filters in place helps to have what I call "bust out" courses in place before the students get into the heart of the engineering curricula.

Moreover, the subject matter taught in DEQ was obsolete a century ago. Nobody seems to give a hoot.

I liked control systems because some modern light brought an onslaught of useful and innovative tools. The irony is that as an expert in control systems, I have bypassed and eclipsed DEQ. In today's world, I stand as a world authority of sorts in differential equations. That would have been hard to predict as it took me four attempts pass DEQ. When I finally did bridge that hurdle, it was Santa Claus who made it happen.

It's hard to second guess all the what-ifs in life. Frankly, I can't even envision what my life would have been like if I had gone on to law school.

I originally intended to remain at Penn State for just one year, into 1965, for my masters, and then go to law school at Michigan in the fall of 1965. That never happened because once I was in the master's program at Penn State, I had better classes and better professors. I liked control systems and eventually decided to go for my PhD in mechanical engineering with a major in control systems.

Cold Engine Car Starting

THERE'S A GREAT STORY about how my grandfather Valdimar Kristensen got a car's engine to start when it was bitterly cold: He would build a fire under it. Grandfather's idea had its merits.

During my early years in Iowa, at times the temperatures would drop to sub-zero figures. So I set out to perfect my own techniques. I kept in my trunk several critical items: a bag of charcoal, some charcoal lighter fluid, and an old garbage can lid. Most everybody in those days had matches or a cigarette lighter.

One time at the Acacia Fraternity house in Iowa City it was extremely cold, about -20 degrees F. Some fraternity guys tried starting their engines, but to no avail.

When I needed to start my engine, I lit the charcoal in the garbage can lid. I knew to not get in a hurry. The charcoal and garbage can lid were about five feet away from my car. I waited for the coals to be well started and just glowing. Of course, by this time my fellow fraternity buddies knew what I was up to. They laughed and said, "You're crazy!"

Because my car was low to the ground, I got out my bumper jack. I jacked the front up about six inches. Then I pushed the pan of glowing coals under the engine. In about ten minutes, I hit the starter. The engine cranked, and started just as if it was summertime. I pulled the garbage can lid out. I lowered the jack.

I was in business. My car was running.

The laughing stopped. Several fraternity buddies asked to be next to slide the glowing coals under their car engines.

This worked dozens of times. No car ever blew up or caught on fire.

Once, Marjorie and I were visiting her aunt and uncle in Mount Pleasant, Michigan. I did the charcoal thing. Marjorie's relatives are still puzzled and pondering just how dumb Dickie was.

I haven't done this in over 40 years. I now have a heated garage. I live in Saint Louis where the temperatures don't get as cold. Newer cars and lubricants do better in cold weather. But it's still fun to think back.

My grandfather also would put a kerosene lantern inside the car's engine compartment the night before.

My Dumbest Professor

THE MECHANICAL ENGINEERING undergraduate curriculum is top-heavy with courses in thermodynamics. Because I had to take so many courses related to thermodynamics, I ended up taking three courses at Penn State from the same professor. This professor was dumb. He took himself and thermodynamics far too seriously.

One day, the professor was describing how densities of fluids can change with temperature. He used gasoline as an illustration. The professor then added the remark (paraphrased), "Because gasoline is more dense at colder temperatures, that is why I buy my gas in the morning."

The problem is that gasoline, even then, was stored in large underground tanks. It is patently absurd to suggest that when gas is pumped in morning hours that it is somehow more dense—and that the buyer is getting more for his/her money. I can assure all that gasoline stored in underground tanks does not see any measurable difference in density depending on time of day.

As an undergraduate, I came to loathe thermodynamics. I could hardly wait to see my thermodynamics courses end.

Ironically, when I first became a professor in the fall of 1968, my very first class assignment was thermodynamics. The course was for electrical engineers who didn't want to be there, but it was required. Moreover, it was statistical thermodynamics, based on probability arguments. Somehow, the students and I survived the semester.

A Hose and 5-Gallon Can

IN APRIL OF 1965, I was in the midst of my master's studies at Pennsylvania State University, close to finishing my master's thesis. Events in my life had shaped circumstances. I had been accepted into the PhD program at Purdue University. Three things coincided: Penn State had a week's break, Marjorie's grandfather had passed in Iowa, and we decided to visit Purdue's campus. We drove west and stayed in a motel somewhere in West Lafayette, Indiana. For some reason, I remember there being a swimming pool at the motel. As it was April, we didn't swim.

After spending the day visiting at Purdue and meeting faculty, we headed further west to Iowa. As I can best recall, our vehicle was a1958 Ford station wagon. It had the dependable Ford 6-cylinder overhead valve engine. In its day, that was a reliable and economical choice in engines.

This was 1965. The Eisenhower national defense highway, now known as the Interstate system, was yet to be completed. We drove on two-lane highways from town to town. After crossing into Illinois, I started to experience car problems. It seemed I had gotten a bad batch of gas containing water, or maybe somebody had dumped some water into my tank. I will never know for certain, but the presence of the water in the motel's swimming pool lingered in my mind.

Somehow, I determined I had water in my gas tank. Being resourceful and having tools along, I unscrewed the tank's drain plug and drained out the water. As I recall, several gallons of water drained out. Upon seeing gasoline flow out, I replaced the tank's drain plug. I had done this after backing the car over a ditch. That gave me room to work under the car's rear without having to jack up the car for clearance.

I started the engine. We were underway again. Unfortunately, the engine didn't run well. It stalled at times, obviously starved for fuel. I did what I could, including stopping to drain out any remaining water. The car would go a quarter of a mile or so and then be starved for fuel. I was stuck. Moreover, it was late by then, about 3 a.m. There were no open gas stations. This was in the days before interstates and 24-hour gas stations.

My situation was clear. I had gas in the tank, but the gas wasn't getting to the engine. Then I got creative. Marjorie and I stopped at a closed gas station somewhere in Illinois. We had about 60 miles to go. In those days cell phones had not been dreamed of, at least not by me. I went behind the closed station. Recall that I was familiar with gas stations and the usual trash behind gas stations. Looking in the trash, I found a steel five-gallon oil can, empty. Next, after again backing over a ditch, I removed the drain plug from the gas tank. I was able to fill the used oil can with gas. Water was not an issue. Gasoline and water have different densities. Water is heavier and drains out first, being at the tank's bottom. The water, if there is any, always drains out first. Once clear gas flows, the rest to come is clear gas.

Coming up with a suitable connecting hose took more resourcefulness.

I again looked in the trash behind the station. Luck was with me—I found a short length of old rubber hose. I placed the filled five-gallon can on the floor in front of the passenger's seat, then snaked the hose through the firewall and into the engine compartment. I disconnected the regular gas line going to the fuel pump mounted on the side of the engine. The hose was then attached to the fuel pump's inlet. I stuck the other end of the hose into the smaller opening in the oil can.

The engine started and ran well. We had sufficient gas to make it to Marjorie's parents' home in Walcott, Iowa. The following day I drove the car to a repair shop. I was later told that the solution was simple. They disconnected the car's regular steel fuel line at the tank. The car was on a lift in their garage. A shot of compressed air did the trick. A glob of something blew out of the gas line. It seemed that the water dumped into my tank in West Lafayette had contained some crud. I asked the shop service guys what the crud looked like, but they told me they couldn't tell as it blew out onto an already greasy floor. I sure hope it wasn't a pile of you-know-what, but if someone was sneaky enough to fill my gas tank with water, I wouldn't put anything past them.

THE GLORY YEARS

Some of the Best, But Still Foolish,
Years of Dumb Dickie's Life
(1963-1981)

Dumb Dickie as a Son-In-Law

WHEN I BECAME the son-in-law in Marjorie's family, some awkward moments followed. After Marjorie and I agreed to marry, I felt obligated to have the customary man-to-man talk with her father. As a dairy farmer, his place of business was when he was milking cows. He was busy but had time to talk. I didn't ask, but rather informed him of our plan to marry.

He responded to my statement, and I paraphrase, "If we lived in Africa, you would have to give me twelve cows."

My response was simple and direct, "We don't live in Africa."

That constituted our discussion. He later told Marjorie that he would give her $1,000 and a ladder. Obviously, an invitation to elope. Marjorie refused. Dad Maxwell had to pay for a wedding. We were married on September 1, 1963. That was a Sunday, in the afternoon. Our schedule was tight, as we needed to be in Pennsylvania bright and early on Tuesday, September 3. That was when Marjorie was to start teaching kindergarten in the small town of Tyrone.

Tyrone was rural and still in the dark ages. Fundamentalist religion was central. Marjorie was told one thing by the school superintendent, "If you choose to drink, do your drinking in some bar other than in Tyrone."

I was trained to be observant and logical. It took me some

time to recognize that not all people prescribe to a pursuit of logic and truth. Some bloopers came from my lips before I had learned this:

- Teachers are bad parents.
- Perhaps the reason the entire family got sick was because the roasted duck had been left out all day (and not refrigerated).
- Where's the food?
- I don't recall seeing any cat skeletons in trees lately.
- Why are we all crammed into a car delivering eggs?

My mother-in-law, Alice L. Kronenberg Maxwell (1916-1985), was an intense lady, a farmer's wife, a mother of six, and a school teacher. I can assure you that my remarks, such as the above, went over like lead balloons.

I once used the farm truck to haul two cows to the sale barn. I could shift the truck's transmission, as it required a skill known as double-clutching. This skill is necessary in larger truck transmissions that don't have synchromesh features. As driver, I had two tasks. First was to load up the two cows. The next task was to hook a chain onto an older car and haul it to a junkyard. One of Marjorie's brothers steered the old car. Upon getting to the junkyard, I crouched down under the rear of the truck to unhook the chain. It was then that one cow decided to urinate. I got doused with a gallon or so of hot cow urine. I had no way to wash or change my clothes.

I once had the opportunity to hunt on the Maxwell family farm and jumped at it. The plan was for Marjorie's younger brother Edwin to go with me, but my father-in-law objected. "But why?" I asked Dad Maxwell.

Dad Maxwell explained that in his youth, one of his high school friends was killed in a hunting accident. Two boys—his friends—had gone to a farm to hunt. Neither of them owned a shotgun so they borrowed some from the farmer. One shotgun was a break-open double-barrel, the other shotgun was a break-open single shot. Both boys wanted the double-barreled shotgun. They settled the matter and hunted for the morning.

At noon, they returned to the house. Both shotguns were set inside the rear door entry. They washed and had lunch.

Upon going out again, both wanted the double-barreled shotgun. Both grabbed for it. A struggle for the gun ensued. One of them had the butt. The other had the muzzle—with the barrels pointed directly at the boy's chest. The boy holding the muzzle ended up losing his grip.

The other boy, holding the butt end, fell backwards. Upon falling backwards, the exposed hammer on one side struck against the doorpost. The shotgun discharged aimed point blank at the other boy's chest. Obviously, the discharge killed the loser of that struggle.

Upon hearing this story, as sad as it was, I responded. The two boys had violated countless rules of firearm safety. I was and am respectful of guns. A gun is a tool, just like a hammer or saw. It is no better or worse than the person using the tool.

- Guns should be loaded only when actively being used.
- When you stop hunting, unload the gun. With a break-open it is easy and can be done in seconds.
- When one isn't hunting, etiquette dictates that break-open shotguns be in the open position.
- Never point a gun at anything you don't intend to shoot.
- Treat and respect all guns as if they were loaded.
- Use only modern firearms with modern safety design features. The older-style gun in his story was grossly unsafe. It should have been deactivated, firing pins removed, and relegated to wall-hanger status.
- Don't ever fight over a firearm. A simple coin toss should suffice.

After explaining the myriad of errors and rule violations the boys had made and demonstrating to my father-in-law that I respected guns and would teach Edwin gun safety, my father-in-law thanked me. He gave me permission to hunt with Edwin and teach him basic gun safety.

At times, I had interactions with my father-in-law involving engineering principles. He once said, "A tractor will have more pulling power when towing something if the chain is shortened." I explained the flaw in his statement. The statement is true only if the chain isn't level. A short chain will yield better towing capacity so long as it is sloped upward. The tensile or pulling load will somewhat lift the object being pulled and will transfer weight or load onto the pulling tractor's rear wheels. The added load gives the pulling tractor more traction. But this only works when the chain is pulling upward. Dad Maxwell pondered that, then thanked me.

All in all, I felt that my in-laws respected me, just as I respected them. Upon my entry into the family, I had been a city kid. I was green when it came to farming and being around livestock. I did learn over the years.

I learned some basic rules about hog loading:
- Give a hog only one way to go: up the chute.
- Never, and I repeat never, allow a hog to turn around and try coming back down the chute.
- Before loading, scatter some shell corn in the truck's bed so the hogs will enjoy the new treat.
- Hogs are smart. Once a hog comes down a chute, you will pay dearly trying to get the hog back up that chute.
- Have all your gates secure and helpers in place before you start moving hogs towards the loading chute.

These are helpful rules in life. Whenever you are in a hog-loading situation, be it hogs or people, give the hogs just one way to go: the way you want them to go.

I did bring certain skills that placed me in high standing, at least in the eyes of Marjorie's younger brothers. I could back up a manure spreader with ease. It's just like backing up a boat trailer. Another skill I had was the ability to splice rope, learned in scouting. One time the hay rope broke. That long rope was used to hoist forked bales of hay into the barn's loft. The rope was pulled by a helper driving a tractor. Normally, my young brothers-in-law would have to wait for their father to return to splice the rope, should it have broken. I did a splice on the spot. That put me, in the brothers' eyes, on a high pedestal.

Because I knew little about farm operations, but much about kitchens, I felt at home in the kitchen with my mother-in-law, Alice Maxwell. I had been a cook in the Army Reserves. I offered to help do the dishes. My mother-in-law smiled. She dubbed me with a new name: Disherella.

Entering Academia

UPON COMPLETION of my doctorate in 1968, I became interested in staying in academia as opposed to going into industry. The reasons were many. Three reasons were June, July, and August. Marjorie, as a teacher, had three months off each summer. I wanted to follow suit.

At first, I anticipated a struggle to find a tenure-track opening. I had presumed that an opening would come up only if some older senior professor phased out of the system. I soon was dealt a dose of reality, combined with some amazing good fortune.

The same year that I graduated from Purdue, the national accrediting board changed the requirements for approval of mechanical engineering curricula. All ME departments nationwide were now mandated to include a required undergraduate course in control systems.

The telephone in our apartment literally rang off the hook. I took five interview trips. Two schools made me offers even without having me interview. In all, seven schools made me offers. Obviously, Herman had been at work.

I became an Assistant Professor at the University of Illinois. One year later, our great summer vacations and excursions commenced.

The year 1969 became a milestone and pivotal year. The booming post-Sputnik era came to a screeching halt, bringing a crash in academia and higher education. Three factors came into play:

1. Man landed on the moon. A Peanuts cartoon with Snoopy said, "If man can reach the moon, why then must I sleep in a doghouse?" The lunar landing was anti-climactic.

2. The Vietnam war protests were having a devastating impact on higher education. Illinois was no exception. Protesting mobs destroyed state property. University budgets were slashed by legislatures.

3. America was beset with racial problems. One minority boy in Marjorie's kindergarten class kept falling asleep in school. Upon asking why, the boy's momma told Marjorie that she made him sleep in a bathtub. Bullets were passing through the thin walls of the public housing project and the bathtub was safer than a bed.

Promises made to me when being recruited in 1968 were swept aside and never honored. The year 1969 brought stark realities home to roost. I was severely impacted by things beyond my control and by things I didn't see coming. It took me years to even grasp what had happened.

Visiting the Grand Canyon

IN THE SUMMER OF 1969, Marjorie and I spent about two months driving out west in a big loop. One stop, although brief, was the mandatory visit to America's Grand Canyon. Like most visitors discover, the Grand Canyon is indeed grand.

I made a Dumb Dickie mistake. I blithely swallowed the conventional wisdom—that the Grand Canyon was the result of millions upon millions of years of ever so slow water erosion. The conventional wisdom claims that the Grand Canyon was cut away one tiny grain of sand at a time.

Upon examining the evidence, I believe the cutting of the Grand Canyon was instead a relatively recent and sudden event. The evidence is overwhelming to affirm the sudden event hypothesis:

1. If water slowly carried grains of sand away, those grains of sand would be deposited downstream when the water rate slowed. There are no build-ups like the Nile and Mississippi deltas or even interior silt flats.

2. If the cutting away of the rock took millions upon millions of years, other natural processes would have softened the canyon's edges and outcroppings. Freezing and thawing of water in exposed crevices over millions of years would have rounded the canyon's side slopes.

3. Large boulders have been discovered several hundred miles downstream. A slowly running river would have never carried boulders, many several feet in diameter, hundreds of miles.

4. If the slow erosion theory held, that process would be universal. Yet the Grand Canyon is unique. There is no similar canyon or geological feature anywhere else on Earth.

5. The Grand Canyon was cut into an elevated plateau of hard rock. Water does not run uphill onto a plateau. A river did not cut the Grand Canyon, but rather the Grand Canyon allowed a river to flow through it after the canyon was cut.

6. The V-shape of the canyon with its narrow bottom suggests a different cutting scenario. The Grand Canyon was cut in a sudden event as a massive deluge of water, and let me suggest ice, burst forth. Yes, I am suggesting a scenario tied in with Earth's changing climate and glaciations.

These are just some of the obvious reasons the slow erosion theory is flawed. The evidence was in front of my eyes, but I was blinded by conventional wisdom. Obviously, if the sudden event hypothesis holds, then many other questions need to be resolved. In other writings, I address this topic and its companion topic— global climate change.

Lessons in Intellectual Property

LESSON ONE. In the summer of 1970, I took a position with a company based in Peoria, Illinois. They made big equipment that was world-renowned and painted yellow. As a staff engineer, I was asked to sit in on a presentation by a vendor. It was your typical dog and pony show. Two guys had a sales pitch, trying to entice Earthworm Tractor Company to purchase their idea or services.

When the presentation ended, I remarked to a senior engineer, Bill, about how impressed I was with the ideas. "Is our company going to take action on any of those ideas?" I asked.

Bill replied, "No, we never do that."

"Then why did we waste our time listening to the presentation?"

Bill answered. "We (Earthworm) have three choices: walk away and don't buy; buy; or lastly, pick their brain so we can take the ideas and run with them ourselves."

Bill informed me that we at Earthworm never do option #2—we never buy. He added that the reason we listened to the vendors was to pick their brains. If Earthworm wanted the ideas, they would put a team of engineers onto it and come up to speed in weeks. Patents were seldom a concern. Earthworm had a room full of patent attorneys able to fight and break virtually any patent. The company would never allow itself to be hostage to an outside vendor. The idea was either good or bad. If Earthworm deemed the idea to be important, they would run with it. Earthworm never bought from some fledgling supplier poised to go out of business at a moment's notice.

Lesson Two. As an outgrowth of my doctoral dissertation, I became partnered with Dr. John R. Cannon, Jr. Cannon was helpful in guiding me towards a critical proof regarding a mathematical theorem. Cannon and I collaborated. We devised a computer algorithm that would allow us to measure the external temperature of an object and compute or predict its internal temperature.

Knowing the interior temperature of a steel ingot is vital in steelmaking. The ingot must be properly hot, but not too hot. Steel manufacturers keep steel ingots in a heated soaking pit. Keeping the ingots there too long is costly as oxidation causes loss of steel.

Cannon and I formed a corporation called HEAT, Inc. We then filed for a patent on our computer algorithm. Intellectual property laws were then changing. Certain computer codes were patentable. After working with a patent attorney, Cannon and I were ready to hit the big time.

We arranged a meeting with a vice president at United States Steel Corporation in Pittsburgh. We did our little dog and pony show. The guy at U.S. Steel said no thanks. He went on to say that he didn't care one bit about our patent. To quote the guy, "We broke Kaiser Steel on their oxygen furnace patent. We'll break you." Cannon and I left U.S. Steel with our tails between our legs and $15,000 poorer. In the early 1970s, my half of the loss represented over six months of income.

I have come to have zero interest in patents. A patent is only a license to sue. You must first be aware of the patent infringement, find a court of jurisdiction, and have the legal budget to endure and prevail. Eli Whitney, inventor of the cotton gin, died in poverty. As cotton mills across the South infringed on his patent, he had to go into each county and file lawsuits. The wheels of justice turn slowly. Most little guys will never see a penny from a patent.

I have become a strong believer in trade secrets and proprietary knowledge. In the adapted bicycling program, my window of time to develop a product spans much longer than the life of a patent. The people who see my adapted bikes continually ask if I have patented the idea. The naïve people who ask that question usually know nothing about patents and intellectual property law—otherwise they wouldn't even waste their well-meaning breath asking.

Lost in the North Woods

EVERY PERSON who has dreamed of adventure at some point must ask a question: What would I do if I ever found myself lost in the woods? That question became far more than academic for me. In the fall of 1971, I went on my third north woods deer hunting trip. The location was Washington Island, Wisconsin, located on the tip of Door County jutting into upper Lake Michigan. The island was about five miles across. Deer were plentiful. I had been told that the deer would eat the locally grown potatoes and acorns. The year before, I had taken a nice eight-point mature buck on Washington Island.

The island had a grass landing strip. To avoid the long drive and the ferry to the island, this year I flew in using my flying club's Piper Cherokee N6237W. I had hunted the prior weekend before Thanksgiving. This was a bonus trip the weekend immediately following Thanksgiving. I had first picked up my brother-in-law Robert in Davenport, Iowa. Bob and I then flew straight to Washington Island. Our friend, guide, and host was Tom Jensen, owner of a motel on Washington Island. Tom picked us up at the airport and took us back to the motel.

Tom wore many hats, one being the game warden. Hunting with the game warden has all sorts of benefits. Other hunters will seldom argue with you. We could hunt on land off-limits to others. When a deer was harvested, Tom's knife was quick in field dressing the animal.

That weekend, just Bob and I were hunting as Tom had other obligations. We lacked sufficient people to drive deer, there being just two of us. As is customary when deer hunting, we arose and ate breakfast early. We wanted to be on our stands before sunrise. Tom loaned us his old pickup truck, and we drove to a cedar swamp he'd shown us the day prior. It was still dark, before dawn. We parked and walked the half-mile from the truck into the swampy area.

Bob took a position a hundred yards or so from me. I selected a place to sit with a backrest. We settled in for a day of waiting. The idea was to just sit quietly all day, in the expectation that a deer would come by. The temperature was slightly below freezing. The sky was overcast. Being in a cedar swamp made it darker yet. A light snow was falling, but with no accumulation. There was little wind to speak of, as the cedars blocked any wind. The snowflakes came seemingly straight down, albeit gently. Tranquil was a word that seemed appropriate.

Sitting on a deer stand in such conditions gives one ample time to commune with nature and to just enjoy being alive. Life doesn't get much better, at least not for somebody who enjoys the freedom of being outdoors in the north woods. This was like being John Wayne, Daniel Boone, Ernest Hemingway, and the Marlboro Man all wrapped up in one.

I had taken my compass bearings going in so that I knew what compass direction to follow whenever it came time to head back to the truck. I sat patiently all day, nibbling on an occasional sandwich. No deer were seen.

As it got later and close to dark, the cedar swamp became enchanted—it was quiet. As darkness fell, the woods around me changed as the images seemed different. I wanted to stay until the last possible minute because deer are most apt to move when darkness comes.

No deer. Upon checking my watch, I saw that the legal hours for hunting had ended. It was time to head back to the truck.

As I removed my compass from my pocket, I discovered that the needle was stuck. I wasn't too concerned. Bob was close by—or so I presumed. I gathered up my gear and made my way towards where Bob had positioned himself. That was a costly mistake. I went towards where Bob had been. Each time I walked a few steps, I had to twist and turn to get over the brush and undergrowth. I had to watch where I walked to not step into water-bogged ground. My boots were leather, not waterproof rubber. I called out to Bob. There was only silence. By then, I had become hopelessly disoriented. Even getting back to my original deer stand was not possible.

My compass was worthless. I had no sense of direction. I needed to go southwest, about 225 degrees. My heart fell. The compass was obviously broken.

Reality dawned on me, or rather hit me over the head like a 2"x4". Without a working compass in a cedar swamp in Northern Wisconsin, I was lost. It was pointless to try walking out. I had lost all sense of direction. I was in a dense undergrowth. Wind didn't help as there was no wind. The option of just walking in a straight line was pointless. Only one direction would take me to high ground and civilization. Most directions would lead me deeper into the cedar swamp and ultimately the cold waters of Lake Michigan. It was now pitch black. There wasn't a sound. At that point, I realized I had to stay where I was and collect my thoughts.

I had heard that lost hunters could fire three consecutive rifle shots as a distress signal. With my .30-30 lever action, I pointed up and fired three shots. Frankly, I was dismayed at how silent three shots can be in a cedar swamp. I next realized that I had to conserve my ammunition. I had about 20 rounds total going in. My box of .30-30 ammunition came with two red plastic belt holders. Each belt holder carried ten rounds. I had to conserve my distress shots. I waited perhaps 10 or 15 minutes, then fired a single shot.

I was making mental provisions as to how I would spend the night alone in a cedar swamp. After about 30 minutes, a wonderful thing happened. I heard a distant truck horn. The horn would blow every few minutes. With each horn blast, I could sense the direction. I set my flashlight onto a tree or object, possibly 10 or 15 feet away. I moved to that object, keeping it illuminated with my flashlight. That assured me I was moving towards the sound of each consecutive horn blast. It was a slow process, but it worked—just so long as the horn blasts kept coming. Again, I waited until the next horn blast. This was not the time for heroic grand leaps. Steady as she goes, goes the old saying.

I had made my way out of the low ground and onto a rise with less undergrowth. With each horn blast I could go a greater distance, about fifty feet. With less undergrowth, my flashlight could illuminate a more distant object. I proceeded to make my way to each targeted object. Feeling more confident, I fired occasional shots, again just one at a time.

Then the horn blasts stopped! Nothing happened for about 15 or 20 minutes. I wasn't terribly worried. I just had to be patient. Even though I was out of the swamp and on firm ground, I wasn't out of the woods yet. I kept calm. I didn't take a step in any direction. I was sure help was on the way. Soon I saw an amazing sight. Tom Jensen was walking towards me with a lantern.

On the way back to the truck, Tom filled me in. "I came home and saw my truck parked there, so I knocked on the door to your motel room. Wanted to see how the deer hunting had gone."

I listened silently, hoping we were almost to the truck.

He continued, "Bob told me you were still hunting. He was

gonna come back for you, but I said I'd go instead." Lucky for me that the first team was in place as opposed to a fledgling rookie.

"But when I got to the pick-up point, I didn't see you. I realized you must be lost."

Tom, with his years of experience, knew to blow the truck's horn. Of all the distress shots I fired, Tom said he only heard one. Upon hearing that shot, he decided to take the truck back to his house to get a lantern. He was going to go into the woods to find me. Being prepared was his first step. That explained why the horn sounds had ceased. Washington Island isn't very big, so Tom came back quickly.

I found my brother-in-law Bob warm and comfortable. He had gotten cold around 2 o'clock. Without bothering to tell me, he walked out of the woods and took the truck back to our motel room. After taking a warm shower, Bob took a nap. All that time I was left alone and uninformed in a cedar swamp sitting on a deer stand.

When I got back to my home in Illinois, I went to an outdoors store. Instead of buying a cheap replacement for my compass, I bought two compasses—both of higher quality. My days of using cheap compasses were over. One compass was the pin-on type. I could sense my direction just by glancing down. I would no longer have to take my gloves off and dig in a pocket. The second compass was larger, like a pocket watch.

From then on, whenever I hunted in unfamiliar territory, it became axiomatic that I carried two compasses. I also tried to pick my hunting companions more wisely. That is far more difficult than buying a compass.

There are many morals to glean from this lost-in-the-woods story. Pick your hunting companions wisely. Always carry two compasses. When you go into unfamiliar territory, carry critical provisions should you have to spend a night or more exposed. Keeping dry is rule #1. A light plastic tarp will do wonders.

Keep your wits—learn to admit you are lost. Recall, all this took place long before cell phones and electronic GPS devices. But be aware that these modern gadgets aren't impervious—they don't always get good reception in remote areas or could become water-soaked if you fall into water.

I'm old-fashioned. I rely on old-fashioned ways. They work when all else fails.

I will tell more about deer hunting, and moose hunting, subsequently.

Island-Hopping in the Bahamas

I OBTAINED my private pilot's license in April of 1968. After moving to Champaign, Illinois later that year, I purchased a membership at EngineAire's Flying Club. The club owned and maintained two Piper Cherokees, N6237W and N8478W. I preferred the '78W aircraft as it had 180 HP and better electronics for communication and navigation. The hourly cost was minimal, then at about $12 per hour. That price included fuel, so it was called "wet."

Airplanes have many advantages over automobile travel. Airplanes can fly in direct lines. Speeds are substantially better than cars, at about 130 MPH. I also enjoyed the absence of speed limit signs. Only in rare instances can one get a ticket for going too fast. Airplanes are not charged highway tolls. There are few traffic lights and stop signs. And, except for landings, there is ample space. One can drift a few hundred feet side-to-side or even up and down. Nobody cares. In the case of automobile driving, if one drifts even a few feet out of the traveling lane, bad things like head-on collisions can happen. It is vastly easier, in the sense of being more relaxing, to fly an airplane than to drive a car.

Airplanes do have a few drawbacks. It is hard to buy fuel while airborne. Weather hazards including icing and thunderstorms can be an issue.

Another advantage for having access to two four-place aircraft was that I had less need for a trip-worthy newer car. For many years, especially when first married and starting out, I managed well driving older cars locally.

With this background stated, I will now tell a story about flying, weather, and gasoline or shortage thereof. The story also brings in my brother Freddie. Recall, it was Freddie who accidentally shot me when I was 15.

This story took place in December 1971. I was 32 years old, an age when life seemed great and filled with adventure.

Freddie was a pilot. At that time he owned his own aircraft, a Piper Comanche retractable. The Piper Comanche was virtually the same size as the Piper Cherokee, but the difference was in the feet. The Piper Comanche's wheels would retract. Cruising speeds were 160 MPH, about 30 MPH faster than my Cherokee 180.

Together, we cooked up a great adventure: to fly together to the Bahamas over Christmas vacation. Marjorie and I were flying in N8478W. Fred and his wife, Suzie, were in Fred's Piper PA-24 Comanche. At the time, neither of us had children. It was just the four of us.

After meeting up at the Fort Lauderdale Airport, we rented the mandatory flotation life rafts and fueled up. The date was December 21, 1971. It was also the winter solstice. We were headed to warmer places, notably the Bahamas. Our first stop was Nassau. Upon landing in Nassau, we cleared Bahamian customs, then spent time shopping and seeing the city. I don't recall specifics, but we did spend the night in a hotel. I am certain of both dates and airports, as these details are documented in my pilot's flight log. Pilots take such records seriously.

The next morning, on December 22, we checked out of our hotel and made our way, I assume by taxi, to Nassau's airport. Our plan was to do some island-hopping. As we prepared to depart, we did the usual things such as checking weather forecasts and refueling. My tendency is to buy fuel whenever I can. This is especially true when two conditions are present. First, when flying out over open ocean in an area where I've never been before. My second green-light for buying fuel is a long paved runway. The airplane will always get in the air given enough runway. Once in the air, I can then burn off some weight in fuel.

As I fueled up, I noticed Fred didn't. I asked about it. He answered, "Oh, I've got plenty of fuel."

We were off and up into the wild blue yonder. Both airplanes had radios. Fred knew more than me about such technical airman things. We could communicate with each other while flying.

We landed on the Island of Eleuthera. Some think that Eleuthera was where Columbus first saw land on his first voyage. After the usual tourist stuff, including swimming and snorkeling, we checked into a hotel. We had dinner. The exchange rates were good. American money was accepted by the locals. We were having a grand time.

The next morning, we checked out of our hotel rooms. It was now December 23, 1971. We were off to do more island-hopping. We couldn't get a weather report in the out-islands of the easterly Bahamas, but the sky looked clear. Again, we were airborne. At some point, instead of heading for Freeport to the north, we turned to head back to Nassau.

That was a great plan except for one problem. As we flew southwest toward Nassau, we could see a serious squall line in front of our desired flight path.

I then got on the radio with Fred. My suggestion was simple. We could fly directly west to Fort Lauderdale Airport. We could thus avoid the squall line. The distance to the Florida coast was a little less than 200 miles. Then Fred came back with his infamous answer: "I don't have adequate fuel to make it that far." I had ample fuel but Freddie didn't.

As we pondered what to do, I started looking at charts and figuring out options. We were then flying at about 6,000 feet above sea level. Upon looking down, I noted a smaller island with an airstrip. We agreed to both land. The name of the island was Grand Berry Cay in the Berry Islands.

Upon landing, we found out that the island was privately owned and upscale. An open shuttle cart took us to the island's hotel. Taking off had ceased to be an option. The squall line was close. Winds were increasing. The sky was darkening. By then, it was also getting late in the afternoon. The winter solstice was accompanied by shorter days, fewer daylight hours. The combination of dark clouds looming, being on a tiny island amidst ocean expanses, few other safe harbors, and lateness in the day all suggested staying on the ground. We were committed to spending the night on Grand Berry Cay. Welcome to the Bahamas!

Everything seemed rosy except for one detail. The upscale hotel had rooms available, but we needed two rooms, being two couples. And the hotel's room rate was US$50 per night per room. For two rooms that came to US$100, plus taxes. I had never paid $50 for a hotel room just to sleep, and I wasn't about to start.

Fred, the two wives, and I huddled. I came up with a plan.

The plan was simple. As per my usual custom, I had a tent and basic camping gear with me. We would camp for the night. We took the shuttle cart back to the airport. Although it was windy, we got into our planes. We taxied to the far end of the runway, which was out of sight of the ground crew people. Both planes were taxied off the runway and we were now ready for our great camping adventure. Nobody on the island was the wiser. We then pitched the tent. We secured the airplanes as best we could. The plan was going well, at least so far.

Then we encountered a few problems. First, the tent was a

three-man tent, not a four-man (or two ladies and two men). Next, Marjorie and I had air mattresses, but Fred and Suzie didn't. Nonetheless, we tried to snooze off, four persons sharing a three-person tent and sleeping on two air mattresses. I don't recall how we solved the blanket problem. I'm certain I had two sleeping bags.

As the night progressed, the winds and rain became intense. Sometime in the middle of the night, the tent stakes pulled out, having been driven into loose sand. The tent collapsed. We got soaked.

As a last resort, all four of us got out of the tent, of course soaking wet. We went back to our respective aircraft. We ended up spending the balance of the night sitting in our aircraft. The airplanes lacked lavatories, so some ingenuity was required. The rain and wind persisted.

With the coming of sunrise, the weather cleared. We organized as best we could and departed for Nassau and a night in a decent hotel. I don't recall refueling on Grand Berry Cay. I had ample fuel, and Fred had enough to make the hop to Nassau, about 30 minutes flight time. We obviously both topped off in Nassau.

On the morning of December 24, we did some additional stupid things. Being bound and determined to island-hop more, we departed Nassau for Freeport on a northern Bahamian island. After touring Freeport, we headed west to Fort Lauderdale. I will continue this flying adventure in the next Dumb Dickie story. Stay tuned.

All of this camping in the rain and wind happened because brother Freddie said, "Oh, I've got plenty of fuel." My brother inherited one trait from our father, Albert Klein. Pop was steadfast in his refusal to buy gas. He preferred to have the bucks in his pocket. When my brothers and I would say that the fuel was getting low, Pop's reply was "We can go from here to Hartford and back on the smell."

We very seldom ever made it to Hartford and back on the smell.

"Call Me Anytime," A Bottle of Cockspur Rum

AFTER FRED AND I and our wives cleared U.S. Customs at Fort Lauderdale International Airport, much of the daylight was behind us. We were back in the air at about three o'clock. We were both headed north flying both planes. Our next charted stop for refueling was Savannah, Georgia. We had a strong preference for bigger airports, as bigger airports have a U.S. Flight Service Station (FSS) on the field. One can walk in, see charts and weather maps, and talk in person to FSS staff. That way, a pilot can get the real dope on weather conditions and forecasts.

Because airplanes have dual controls, unlike most cars, I was able to get an hour or so of shut-eye. Marjorie had taken some flying lessons, and even soloed. She agreed to fly some easy stretches as we followed the Florida coastline headed north. When we could, we flew over ocean but kept land in sight. That also allowed us to shorten our distance as we passed Jacksonville. It is called cutting the corner.

Fred and Suzie landed in Savannah before Marjorie and me. Fred waited on the ground for us to arrive in our slower airplane. Upon refueling, I suggested that Fred and Suzie put on some speed and get to wherever home happened to be. I recall them living near Baltimore at the time. The date was December

24, 1971. It was Christmas Eve.

Marjorie and I were going farther, to Bridgeport, Connecticut. It was dark when '78 Whiskey lifted off. We were headed for the next refueling stop, Richmond, Virginia. It would be a long day of flying for me—in fact the longest ever.

I had decided on Richmond because it was at about my fuel range limit, and the Richmond Airport was listed as having 24-hour refueling. Smaller airport FBOs (fixed base operators) close up at night. I knew we would be landing in Richmond close to midnight.

As we flew north, the headwinds picked up. Our ground-speed was diminishing. This meant a longer flight time, but my available fuel supply was fixed. Airplanes have fuel gauges, but pilots trust the clock over a fuel reading. At cruise speed, the Cherokee burned about 11 gallons per hour. The Cherokee has two tanks, one in each wing. The total tank capacity was 50 gallons, but in aviation lingo, not all is usable. After 4 hours and 15 minutes, getting on the ground becomes critical.

My problem was clear. I was hitting headwinds that slowed me down. I had to make a critical decision: either put down at some smaller airport without fuel service, or stretch it and get into Richmond—"on the smell," to paraphrase my father. It was a clear night. I could see the lights of Richmond ahead of me. I chose to head on to Richmond.

I landed at Richmond and taxied to the FBO. The problem was that, being Christmas Eve, the FBO attendant had been given the night off. Nobody was there to refuel '78W.

The Flight Service Station (FSS) was open, being governmental. A call was made. An employee graciously got out of bed, came to the airport, and topped us off. The tanks were so low that '78W took on 43 gallons. I assumed I was down to my last usable five gallons of fuel: about thirty minutes of flight time. That was cutting it close, especially as it was dark, I was less than fresh, and I was not familiar with the area.

I was grateful to the FBO attendant, a smiling and helpful African-American man. Then, I recalled that in Nassau, I had purchased two bottles of an exotic and hard-to-obtain rum: Cockspur Rum from the Island of Barbados. Our rear seat was crammed with our gear and things. I reached back and pulled out a bottle.

I handed the bottle to the guy. He was indeed happy. With a big smile he said words that will remain with me forever, "Call me anytime."

It was now several hours into Christmas Day, but still night. We lifted off headed towards Bridgeport, Connecticut. The headwinds were severe. I estimated a headwind of about 40 knots "on the nose" at cruising altitude. Because of headwinds, it was better to fly lower. On the leg to Bridgeport, I flew at about 3,000 feet AGL (above ground level). Other than Santa Claus on his sleigh, there was virtually no other traffic.

My next problem was the controlled airspace, similar to an inverted wedding cake, for Kennedy International Airport. Regulations prohibited VFR (visual flight rules) traffic, and I was a VFR pilot. I contacted the Kennedy Approach Control on the frequency given by the ATIS (Automated Terminal Information Service) radio recording. The controller assigned me a four-digit transponder code for my aircraft. That way, I was positively identified on approach control radar. I was first told that I had to climb in altitude to be over 6,000 feet if I wanted a direct flight through Kennedy's controlled airspace. Fortunately, I explained my situation and requested that he clear me to cross over and through JFK's airspace at my current altitude of 3,000 feet. I explained that I wasn't a concern to traffic as he had no other traffic at that wee hour. The flight controller, technically referred to as "approach control," granted my request. I was cleared to fly through Kennedy's controlled airspace. Instead of calling me "Seven-Eight-Whiskey," he called me "Seven-Eight-Jingle Bells."

After passing over Kennedy, I was approaching Bridgeport's Igor Sikorski Memorial Airport. As a technical note, the airport was located in Stratford, where my parents lived. The tower was closed at that hour, so I communicated with the FSS located on the field. Since the tower was closed, I was responsible for myself. I did not need a clearance to land. Instead, I was in charge as per visual flight rules. The FSS guy was merely helping me by providing a constant updating on surface winds, both speed and direction.

While I was on the radio with Flight Service, I was told that a local ordinance prohibited night usage of a certain runway as the noise bothered local residents. I had to land on the authorized runway. My problem was the matter of attempting a cross-wind landing given strong cross-wind conditions. Recall, it was dark. I had been flying that day for fifteen hours. The FSS guy called out the wind speeds and directions as I approached the runway. We had agreed that I would make the approach and decide at the last second whether to land or go around to try again. The game plan was to attempt to land when the winds abated or changed to a better direction. On the first approach, I managed to land safely. Put in other words, I didn't land the airplane but instead flew it onto the runway. I was at a speed above stall speed. This afforded me better control of the airplane. Once my wheels were on the runway, I released the flaps, thus assuring less lift.

After taxiing in and securing the airplane with tie-down ropes, I called my parents to come and pick us up. It was dark. It was about five o'clock in the morning, Christmas Day.

Oddly, I think I still have the second bottle of Barbados Cockspur Rum. It remains unopened after some 47 years. Perhaps a day will come when it can be opened.

I wish to comment on pilot jargon. Flying requires communications. The communications must be brief and leave no room for confusion. In telling these flying stories, I have tried to use proper terminology, the type of terminology that pilots use, expect, and rely upon. There is no room for sloppiness or misinterpretation. To that I say "affirmative."

Canoeing in the Boundary Waters

WHEN I WAS AN ARMY RESERVIST in the early 1960s, a fellow reservist, Sgt. John Bolton, showed me photographs of his canoe trip into Quetico's Boundary Waters. I carried that dream, waiting for the opportunity to partake in my own Boundary Waters adventure.

My dream became a reality in the summer of 1972. Five people made that adventure come true. In addition to Marjorie and me, the other three were family members on Marjorie's side. As an active pilot, I opted to pilot N8478W from Davenport,

Iowa, to Ely, Minnesota. Yes, five of us plus our gear squeezed into the ever-faithful workhorse, my flying club's four-seater Piper Cherokee 180.

As we prepared for the trip, we agreed we would jointly keep a running diary. The diary, which tells of the never-ending confusion and disorganization of the trip, is too lengthy to be included in this volume. However, it will be reproduced in its entirety in a separate volume.

I will inject that I was the only one of the five mighty and fearless adventurers who had ever been in a canoe before the trip's start. Of course, the other four thought themselves experts and skilled canoeists. They knew everything, and even argued their opinions with vigor. All sorts of mishaps beset us, one being that we were struck by a lightning bolt.

R. E. Klein vs. the KGB

AFTER MY DAUGHTER, VICTORIA, was born in 1973, I was gathering steam in my professional pursuits. Early in 1974, or possibly late in 1973, feeling altruistic, I initiated paperwork to invite a Soviet scholar to the University of Illinois. I felt I could do my little part in softening Cold War tensions.

That was indeed a stupid thing to attempt.

The Soviet scholar arrived sometime in January or February of 1974. His first name was Sergei. He was roughly the same age as me, in his thirties. As I recall, he said he was married and had one son. I don't recall him ever showing me photographs of his wife and son. He came from deep within Russia, from the city of Irkutsk. That city is located on the banks of Lake Baikal, a lake that is massive mostly because of its depth. Lake Baikal has more fresh water in it than all other freshwater lakes in the world combined. Although Sergei was from deep inside Siberia, he was white-Russian. His father had been a Soviet military officer, assigned to live in Irkutsk. I assumed that Sergei's father served in the Soviet Red Army in World War II. Sergei spoke halting English. I was able to communicate sufficiently with him.

Sergei came to a few of my class lectures, but after several weeks he kept to himself. I interacted with him more socially as opposed to professionally. His engineering background was mostly in vibrations. He appeared to know some applications related to helicopter vibration management techniques. I never saw a hint of any deep interest in engineering, computing, or mathematics. I tended to be polite and give him the benefit of the doubt. I let him do his thing, as I had a heavy research and teaching schedule.

After several weeks, an FBI agent knocked on my office door and introduced himself. "We are interested in Sergei. As a guest in our country, we want to assure that no unfortunate incident occurs." The agent then explained that he wanted to meet periodically with me. He asked that I come to his office, located near campus. I did for a while.

Soon after, the FBI agent suggested we meet at a neutral location. We started to meet twice weekly. The meeting place was in a rear room of a Holiday Inn, then located in Urbana, Illinois. Our twice-weekly meetings had evolved into long and detailed debriefing sessions. Each meeting typically lasted several hours. I was asked all sorts of questions, for which I usually had the answers. The agents inquired about the type of shoes Sergei wore. They asked what was playing on the radio or television in his apartment. They asked about his diet and drinking habits. Of course, Russians drink straight vodka that is kept in the freezer compartment. Whenever I visited Sergei at his modest apartment, I had to consume a glass of straight vodka. When I say a glass, I mean perhaps six ounces. That was straight vodka, so this was serious drinking.

As time went by, it was obvious that the FBI had interests far beyond avoiding an "unfortunate incident" as they'd called it. "So are you really this concerned about Sergei being the victim of an incident?" I asked. I had to know more. "What is it... do you think he'll be robbed on a street at night?"

"We just want to know Sergei better," an agent replied. The FBI explained that Soviet scholars often go back to Russia and later rise to positions of power. Our national interests were served if we knew more about men like my guest Sergei.

Next, I was introduced to a CIA operative, who began to attend our bi-weekly debriefings. At one point the FBI/CIA team requested that Marjorie and I host a social gathering at our home. The objective was to permit a lady to appear as Marjorie's cousin and to accidentally meet Sergei. I assumed that the lady, who was attractive and yet professional, was a prostitute working for the FBI/CIA. Whatever happened happened, as Sergei told me at the gathering that "Linda" was giving him a ride home.

I once drove Sergei to see some of Champaign County where I owned a farm acreage. We stopped and got out. I like guns. I took out a small pistol, a Walther Model PP semi-automatic. We shot at some tin cans. Sergei was pretty adept at shooting. This certainly wasn't his first time handling a firearm. I never said anything to the FBI, but I kept Sergei's adeptness and skill with firearms in the back of my mind. I take firearms seriously; I don't forget when I see somebody consistently hitting targets.

Things became increasingly intertwined and complex. By then, Sergei and I had become more at ease with each other. He started to suggest that I come to the Soviet Union, to tour and to give some engineering lectures. Sergei excitedly suggested that he had friends who would get me some fine rugs. He was speaking of Oriental hand-woven rugs from within Soviet areas close to the Middle East. Sergei also assured me that he had hunter friends who would give me a "bearfur." I later realized that he was offering me a Siberian bear skin rug, the type with the head still on that filled a standard-sized room. I informed the FBI/CIA about Sergei's invitation to visit a string of cities and universities in the Soviet Union, and they were pleased. They encouraged me to accept.

After about five or six months, in late June or early July of 1974, Sergei told me that he had accepted an invitation to go to

Boston to interact at M.I.T. By coincidence, I was planning to go to Buffalo, New York to visit a civil engineering colleague and tour his facility. The civil engineer was Dr. T. T. "Larry" Soong at the University of Buffalo. I was then planning on visiting my parents who were living in Stratford, Connecticut. As a private pilot, I planned to fly there in my flying club airplane, the trusty four-seater Piper Cherokee, N8478W. The four persons in my airplane were Marjorie, her younger sister Mary, my then year-old daughter Vicki, and me as pilot.

I flew from Bridgeport to Norwood, Massachusetts, an airport located near Boston, on July 10, 1974. My preference was to use smaller airports with lax traffic control, as opposed to dealing with congested large airports like Boston's Logan International Airport. In 1974, I was still a VFR pilot, flying under visual flight rules. A year later in 1975, I qualified for my instrument flight rules (IFR) rating. My family and I landed at Norwood on a Wednesday. We got a rental car and checked into a hotel. I was set to connect with Sergei the following day, Thursday, July 11. The objective, as set up by my FBI contacts, was to hand Sergei off to a new contact, somebody from the Boston area FBI office. The plan was bring along a "friend" of mine who just happened to bump into me on the street, but who was actually an FBI plant.

By this time, I realized this was a deeply-rooted game of espionage and intrigue. In briefings with the FBI before leaving Illinois, I had been informed that Sergei was a suspected Colonel in the KGB, a master Soviet spy. His target was what is called Route 128. In America, especially at that time, much of our electronic technology was rooted in spin-off high-tech companies from M.I.T. origins.

In the morning, my family and I drove to an address the FBI had given us where we picked up Sergei. It was some sort of secure rooming house. We were never invited in.

The FBI had given me a code name to use upon calling their

office in Boston. However, the FBI branch office in Boston was inept. They dropped the ball. My "old friend" never showed up as planned. I made a few excuses to use a pay telephone to reestablish contact with the Boston FBI office. I never made physical contact. I now had a Russian spy sitting in my car's backseat and nothing to do.

I suggested to my family and Sergei that we drive out on Cape Cod to see the sunset. As a kid I had gone on numerous Cape Cod family vacations. I was familiar with Cape Cod and its beaches. Upon reaching a state park beach near Orleans, the sight of the ocean overwhelmed Sergei. After rushing out of the car, he undressed down to his shorts. He ran ahead of us and dove into the Atlantic. Recall that Sergei was a Russian from Siberia. He loved swimming in cold water. Unfortunately, we had no towels along. It was also late and dark. The sun had long set.

Sergei sat in the backseat shivering. He and I stopped at a tavern. He had his customary drink of vodka. That must be how Russians warm up.

The drive back to Boston took the better part of an hour. I'm sure we stopped somewhere for food, but those details have slipped from my memory. As we approached Boston to take Sergei back to his rooming house, it was past midnight. I was driving. Marjorie was sitting up front trying to read the map in the dark. I ended up taking a wrong turn. We were somewhere in South Boston—in the dark. Anybody who has ever lived in or driven in Boston knows that Boston is in a league by itself. Recall that in 1974 GPS and smart phone technology existed only in the Dick Tracy comics. We were hopelessly lost.

As Marjorie and I tried to figure out where we were, Sergei started giving us right, left, and straight directions. He was in the dark. He had no map. He had never been in Boston before, except for several days immediately following his arrival. On top of all this, the accidental wrong turn had come as a total surprise.

Now came the moment of truth. Sergei took us through about 20 turns and never made a mistake. I could accept that Sergei had a photographic memory of Boston's street layout, but it was obvious that he recognized our location based on buildings as opposed to street signs.

We dropped Sergei off at his rooming house. The next day, on Friday, July 12, I went to see him as planned. Somebody answered the door and said that Sergei wouldn't be there today. I never saw him again, although months later I did get a book in the mail about Siberia. That book arrived with no letter, but it was autographed. I still have that book.

My family and I had a final debriefing meeting with the FBI and CIA on Friday, July 12, 1974. We departed Norwood Airport and flew south the short distance to Newport, Rhode Island. The meeting took place at an upscale restaurant in Newport. There were several FBI and CIA agents present, plus my family. I had never met any of these agents before. I was told that they were not associated with the Boston FBI office.

"You know, I must say I'm disappointed about being left standing on a corner in Boston," I said. "Your agent never showed up."

"Yeah, sorry about that," one of the agents said. "Those Boston agents have a track record of goofing up."

Perhaps they had gotten lost after making a wrong turn.

Over dinner I finally got some answers that made sense. The American game was to recruit Sergei to become a double-agent—an agent working for us. The method of recruiting a double-agent was to analyze the person and determine their weaknesses or points of vulnerability. In Sergei's case, his weaknesses were a love of beautiful women and a love of beautiful music. Yes, true Russians are deeply romantic. True Russians love Russian music. Oddly, Sergei had identified my own weakness, at least one of them. I loved beautiful furniture, fine oriental rugs, and such. That is why he had tempted me with a massive Siberian bear skin rug and fine Middle Eastern rugs.

"So how was Sergei able to navigate in the dark through what must have been several miles of twisted Boston streets?" I asked.

The agents did not seem surprised. They explained that the Soviets placed such emphasis on penetrating Boston that they had built a model city that duplicated Boston. Sergei was able to navigate Boston in the dark even though he had only been in Boston two days and hadn't had access to a car.

When I'd earlier told the FBI/CIA that Sergei had invited me to Russia, they were in favor of my accepting. That night over dinner, one of the agents casually dropped the following line: "Oh, by the way, we would like you to do a few small jobs while there." It was then that I dropped them like a hot potato.

I am patriotic and would gladly do such small jobs for my country, but six factors chilled me.

1. The FBI and CIA never came clean. It had taken me about half a year of intrigue and risk to finally get them to tell me exactly what I was up against and why.

2. I realized that even our FBI and CIA are mortal and have imperfections. The Boston office of the FBI appeared grossly incompetent. Note that Robert Mueller, the Special Counsel who investigated President Trump in 2017 – 2019 built his career in the FBI's Boston office.

3. My intuition smells a dirty and far deeper plot. Recall, significant counterplots have been unveiled since then. Six FBI agents were taking payoff bribes from organized crime. Four innocent men were sentenced to life imprisonment for a 1965 murder. Courts, decades later, released two of the four men. The men were awarded a settlement of $110M. The other two innocent men languished and died in prison prior to the court's reversal. I was in Boston while much of this was going on. My

sinister mind senses a connection. Could it have been that my keen nose didn't want to come into contact with corrupt FBI agents?

4. I am a daring but also cautious individual. Just as the FBI and CIA studied Sergei, I had to assume that the KGB had studied me. I was a known person to them. I would never and have never traveled behind what was then the Iron Curtain.

5. My paternal grandfather, John F. Klein (1883-1968), was a Russian citizen by birth. In America in 1913, in his naturalization request, he denounced Czar Nicholas and his Russian birth citizenship. Oddly, an obscure Soviet law stated that such persons and their issue were still considered as Soviet/Russian citizens. If I ever set foot in Russia or the Soviet Union, that law could be invoked and applied to me. I had no interest in going to Russia and never being seen again.

6. My instincts warned me of a pending trap. I was being offered things that were too good to be true. My weakness was my affinity for exotic and beautiful material possessions. Sensing a trap, I went cold turkey. I ceased to covet and acquire fine treasures. Not only did I refuse the invitation to travel to Russia on a speaking tour, I also changed my domestic spending habits. I cut back immensely on purchases of fine things like antique furniture, art treasures, sterling, and finery in general. I was never again tempted to acquire a massive Siberian bear skin rug.

At the conclusion of the dinner in Newport, my family and I flew back to Bridgeport's Igor Sikorsky Airport. We stayed that night with my parents in Stratford. I submitted a statement to the Champaign FBI contact with a summary of my out-of-pocket expenses for the Boston portion of my trip. As I recall, I was reimbursed in cash, never by check.

As an aside, I was told at that dinner that Sergei had entered my home in Champaign and had stolen something.

"I don't recall a forced entry. Or a theft," I said.

"He stole a set of keys off your desk at the university," one of the agents said. "Then he used the keys to enter your house."

A lightbulb went off. "Yes! I lost a set of keys a while back. I didn't think anything of it at the time. I didn't even remember it until now! Why didn't Sergei use the keys and then slip them back onto my desk? Or maybe let me find them on the floor?"

"A professional spy would never risk returning something he stole."

Interesting. "So what did he steal from me?"

"Something quite valuable," the agent replied. "Pictures of your wife and daughter."

Sergei used my identity to present himself as Richard Klein. The FBI/CIA assumed that Sergei could switch language style and make himself totally American at whim.

"What was worth sending a KGB spy to the University of Illinois?" I asked. I couldn't imagine.

I was told that my value to the KGB was twofold. First, I served as a stepping stone. Sergei used me and my invitation to gain entry into America and then to get to Boston. The target was always the high-technology industry located on Route 128 that circles Boston. The second benefit of KGB master spy Sergei going to Illinois was the opportunity for him to become familiar with me and learn all sorts of things about my life. With that information as well as critical documents stolen from me, Sergei was able, like Superman stepping into a telephone booth, to pass himself off as an American, a professor from the University of Illinois. Sergei knew all he needed to know about me, and even kept the stolen pictures of my wife and daughter in his wallet as he pretended to be R. E. Klein. Sergei stole the most valuable thing of all: my identity and even my family. It was incredibly dumb of me to be taken advantage of. This also explains why the FBI and CIA agents were continually asking me about Sergei's mannerisms, food preferences, how he combed his hair, how he tied his shoelaces, and such.

I was useful to the FBI and CIA. They knew Sergei's game and what he was doing. I wasn't told because I didn't need to know. The FBI and CIA had a more ambitious goal—to recruit Sergei into becoming a double-agent. That game is high risk, but if successful, the rewards are immense. Having an agent within the KGB but working for our side provides incredible information helpful to us. The double-agent is working for them, but deeply hidden is the agent's value as he is really working for us.

At the final debriefing dinner in Rhode Island, once the picture emerged, other seemingly odd things began to make sense. One was that Sergei always had a radio or television turned up loud in his apartment. Sergei once called the radio his "constant companion." The FBI/CIA explained that loud background noise affords the spy protection from wire taps and hidden microphones or "bugs." Next, the only books Sergei had were Ian Fleming's James Bond 007 spy novels. I am now convinced that he read these so that if he ever got caught, he could claim to just be playing a pretend role as "007."

As the FBI/CIA always reimbursed me for my out-of-pocket expenses in cash, I had no way to prove my involvement with any of this. I then proceeded to install a modern security system in my home in Champaign. Home invasion had become quite real for me.

As I typed this spy-thriller story some 44 years after the fact, one interesting question has arisen for me to ponder. When in all this process did the good guys on our side decide to shoot the works and attempt to recruit my Soviet guest to become a double-agent? My reasoning suggests that the decision was made mid-stream. That is to say after I had become involved. Our players had to know some things about Sergei and a bundle about me. If my conjecture is correct, that implies that I had become a valuable and even key piece in this giant high stakes chess game. Fortunately, I will never answer that question with certainty.

Two witnesses are still around 44 years later who can affirm some details: Marjorie and her younger sister, Mary. My daughter, Victoria, was along during the Boston adventures, but she was one year old at the time. Interestingly, the FBI and CIA agents took an interest in Marjorie's younger sister. At our dinner meeting, they threw out the suggestion that Mary consider becoming an FBI agent. At the time she was an elementary school teacher. The agents made it clear: The best agents are those who are from another line of work. Mary could pretend to be an elementary school teacher because she *was* an elementary school teacher. Mary was obviously flattered, but I have no knowledge that she ever became an agent working for the FBI. I recently asked her. She laughed and said "no." But of course, top agents are so good that nobody discovers their real purpose or role.

Now comes Richard Klein. The FBI and CIA are masters at flattery. The legendary longtime FBI head, J. Edgar Hoover, had just stepped down. The agents at the final debriefing chatted with me, telling me that they had found their new FBI head— none other than yours truly. In the six or eight months of interacting with me as an operative, the FBI and CIA agents came to have deep respect for me. When asked about what kind of socks and underwear Sergei wore, I was able to answer in incredible detail. If I had ever traveled into the Soviet Union as a spy, I could have been immensely worthwhile. With my engineering background, I could see details such as electrical transmission lines, traffic patterns, crowd densities at train stations, and countless other things. I had an eye for noting and understanding detail. The Soviet Union had been closed to western travel and eyes for close to a lifetime. My invitation to travel included places deep inside Russia, such as the hidden city of Irkutsk along with transit on the trans-Siberian railway.

In my estimation, I was up against a master KGB spy. Sergei was good at his job, but I consider myself to have been his equal or better.

Sergei made at least three mistakes that revealed he was far different than someone in the role of a visiting Soviet scholar:

- He showed only superficial interest in academic and scholarly pursuits. Other than attending a few of my class lectures, he soon displayed no interest in mathematics and engineering.

- When I took him out to see the countryside and pulled out my classic James Bond style Walther, he did not feign ineptness in shooting skills. Instead, he handled the Model PP with skill and dexterity. Clearly, Sergei was trained in marksmanship. James Bond preferred the Walther Model PPK, but my Model PP was similar only in .32ACP as opposed to James Bond's preferred .380 (a shortened version of the 9mm Lugar Parabellum).

- Sergei demonstrated a great ability to navigate Boston's bizarre streets even in the dark, while in the backseat. I consider this third breach to be beyond any debate. It was highly improbable that Sergei could randomly make turn decisions to go several miles in Boston and end up at his precise address. The probability of him making random choices and being correct would be akin to buying one ticket and winning the power-ball jackpot. In mathematical terms, he made about 20 consecutive decisions, each involving three choices as we approached each intersection: Go right, left, or straight. The odds of not making a mistake were one in three raised to the 20th power (3^{20}). He did this astonishing feat with absolutely no prior warning. I assume that he dropped his cover merely because he was cold, wet, tired, and anxious to be back in his room and rid of Marjorie and me.

I can never say for certain, but I consider myself to have been his better. In his shoes, I would have never made such obvious blunders. My assessment was that as a Soviet KGB agent, he was filled with arrogance. He presumed that Americans are stupid. In his mind, he had no need to maintain total consistency in outward appearances. Sergei seriously underestimated me, my intelligence, and my powers of observation. (Yes, I can be arrogant too.)

America eventually won the Cold War—because we were more economically efficient than the Soviets. Sergei's vast underestimation of me was to my advantage. Perhaps I missed my calling in life.

"Why I Don't Wear Underwear"

IN THE FALL OF 1974, I arranged a trip for two engineering faculty colleagues and me to go moose hunting in Geraldton, Ontario. Jim Leach, an older and crusty guy, had hunted there before. He had several sets of moose antlers hanging outside his backyard shop building in Urbana, Illinois. Years earlier, Jim had befriended a French-Canadian logger, Alphonse, so we had the invitation and the place. The third hunter was Dick DeVor. DeVor, born in 1944, was five years younger than me. He was from Wisconsin and had a long history of deer hunting.

My dream was to go with these two seasoned hunters. This dream included driving 24 hours straight from Illinois to Geraldton. I had considered flying in a club airplane, but the airplanes available to me weren't up to the job. We were three heavy guys with too much gear. If I ever landed up north, snow might fall and close the airport. Canadians in remote areas don't plow runways, but instead resort to skis on aircraft. I wasn't ready to take that risk. And if we did get a moose, we wouldn't be able to fit a moose into a four-seater airplane.

I have countless stories I could tell about my great Canadian moose hunting trip, but I'll stick to just a few.

Jim Leach was an incredible person and good friend. His stories and accomplishments are legend. Leach had served as an

Air Force bomber pilot during WWII. He had traveled all over the world, notably Africa and India. His expertise was in foundry. In his world travels he taught local peoples the basics of foundry and metal casting. India and Africa thirsted for that knowledge.

If you told a story about fighting tigers in India with Hemingway, Jim Leach had one better. He had fought tigers side by side with Rudyard Kipling. I'm exaggerating, of course, but please accept my point. Once at a dinner party at Leach's home, Jim got out a snake skin from India that was perhaps 20 feet long when unrolled. If you dared to match your snakeskin story against Jim's, you would surely lose.

We set out in Jim's new Ford F-250 with four-wheel drive. Jim had just purchased it. He paid for the truck by counting out hundred dollar bills. Jim never had a credit card. He never had a mortgage. He paid cash for everything. If you never use credit, you don't have a credit score or rating. How many people do you know who have never bought anything on credit?

We pulled an army surplus utility trailer behind us. You had to have a trailer to bring your moose home.

As we left, Jim's wife Mary Jane handed us a large tin of fresh-baked chocolate chip cookies. The tin of cookies was to last the week. It was empty inside of 50 miles. I got mildly constipated because of the change in my diet.

As we drove, Jim said to DeVor and me, "Because we will be together for a week, I want to tell you why I don't wear underwear."

DeVor and I were speechless. We tried to utter that we weren't curious or concerned. Jim persisted.

He explained that when he was a boy in Lawrenceville, Illinois, he had been walking on the top of a wooden picket fence. He fell and became impaled on a fence picket. After being lifted off and treated, his cheek glands that normally lubricate the cheeks didn't work. Jim Leach said that he didn't wear underwear so that his cheeks could get better ventilation.

When we finally passed Duluth and crossed the Canadian border, we decided to buy our Ontario moose hunting licenses. We still had eight hours to go, but if we saw a moose along the way, we wanted to be able to shoot it. We were in Ontario, so our licenses would be good for all our time in Canada.

We encountered a problem. Ontario had passed a law saying that hunting licenses were sold only to persons who had passed a hunter safety course. There was an exception. Licenses could be sold if the person could produce a hunting license that had been issued earlier. This was the grandfather clause in the law.

Jim Leach and I both were able to dig out a past hunting license from our wallets. Dick DeVor had hunted in Wisconsin. Unfortunately, he didn't have an old license with him.

The clerk suggested that we turn around and drive back to Minnesota. DeVor could buy a Minnesota hunting license. That would allow him to qualify for the Ontario license.

As I observed this, the suggestion to backtrack hundreds of miles seemed repugnant and foolish. I am reminded of the line in Patton's opening speech in the movie of the same name, "I don't like paying for real estate twice." In our situation, backtracking required that we cover the same real estate three times. I asked if it would be possible for DeVor to stop at a Ranger or Royal Canadian Mounted Police station. He could take and pass a test on the spot. This made sense as DeVor was smart. He had hunted all his life. He even had a PhD in mechanical engineering. Based on my suggestion, we kept driving north.

At Thunder Bay, a large city by remote backwoods standards, we located a ranger station. Leach and I waited in the truck. DeVor came out with some bad news—he had flunked the test! The ranger had asked DeVor to handle a rifle. DeVor turned with the firearm and swept it by, thus pointing it at the ranger. Of course, DeVor claimed he didn't, but the ranger made the decision and it was final. DeVor had flunked.

In the truck, we collected our thoughts. Should we now drive 300 miles back to Minnesota? We didn't want to go backward when we could be going forward. Certainly, there would be another ranger station ahead. We drove on.

Way north of Lake Superior, near Lake Nipigon, we found another ranger station. We had gotten a hunter safety book from the first ranger. I grilled DeVor as we drove, going over the rules and how to pass the test. DeVor managed to pass the test on the second try. We proceeded into Geraldton, Ontario.

Alphonse said, "We get a moose for sure."

We never did. We only saw two moose while driving along a highway. We stopped to get our rifles out.

"No," Alphonse said, "We are in a no-hunting preserve."

In addition to Alphonse, his nephew came along. Alphonse's wife was native Cree Indian, as was the nephew. The Indian carried a British Enfield bolt action in .303 British. Those guns were war surplus and cost little.

What surprised me was that the nephew carried a small .22 rifle over his shoulder. I inquired as to what good it does to shoot moose with a .22? I was told that the .22 was used to shoot whatever came by, such as a possum or porcupine. These people were subsistence hunters. They shot anything that would fit into the pot.

Alphonse had logged for Kimberly-Clark all his working life. He never had to go beyond 20 miles from his home to cut trees. From that day on, I never worried about conserving paper. God made Canada and all those trees—just so I could express my ideas on paper. I just grab another sheet of paper whenever needed.

Our Canadian hosts were impressed with several things. First was my two compasses, including the pin-on.

The second thing they remarked on was my rifle. It was a standard Remington Woodsmaster 740 semi-auto in .30-06. The scope was a Weaver K-4. Several years earlier I had cut and fitted rubber hoods to extend forward and back. The purpose was to keep the telescopic scope lenses protected and dry. That seemed to impress them. Recall, I am talking about seasoned Canadian loggers and hunters, people who really knew and who had lived the game.

After about three or four days of hunting, at one lunch break I asked Jim Leach if I could look at his rifle. All of us had .30-06 rifles. All had scopes. To my dismay, Leach's scope lenses were covered with mist. It seemed that Jim had wanderlust. Instead of remaining on a stand waiting for moose, he opted to walk. Leach explained that he preferred to walk mile upon mile on logging trails, never sitting down. Perhaps the ventilation on his cheeks was better. Walking along slowly was his way of moose hunting. He just hoped that he and a moose would stumble upon each other.

The problem was that Jim carried his rifle over his arm, thus exposing the scope to the elements. That day a light mist was falling. Because of the mist, his rear lens was blurry. Jim could not have shot a moose if one had appeared. He walked the whole time in the mist and never looked at his scope. He didn't seem bothered. He explained that way of hunting was exactly how he had shot moose during his prior hunting trips.

I asked Alphonse what to do if I ever became lost. The answer was simple. Use your compass and go north. After you go about 20 miles, you will come to the trans-Canadian railway track. Turn east. In about 50 miles you will come to a town, Nakina. Three points were vividly obvious:

- Don't get lost.
- Should you get lost, don't expect somebody to find you.
- The two points above should have been obvious. That's why I wasn't told until I was dumb enough to ask.

I was doubly sure to not do anything stupid such as getting lost.

Because we pulled a utility trailer, I felt comfortable bringing along a few extra things. One item was a chainsaw with gas.

DeVor thought that was a little extreme. Well, on our very first morning as we traveled along a logging trail, we came upon a fallen tree across the trail. With the chainsaw we had it cut and removed in no time. DeVor never again questioned my caution and advance planning. Another useful extra was a come-a-long and some chains. Because Jim Leach's truck was showroom-new and spotless, he drove it through some soft ground at a creep, not a roar. When a four-wheel drive is stuck, it's really stuck. We had to use the come-a-long to get it unstuck.

As Alphonse placed us on stands, he gave us some instructions. If a cow and calf come into sight, first shoot the calf. The cow will run away, but will soon come back to the calf. Then shoot the cow.

Alphonse instructed us what to do if we shot a moose. Do not attempt moving it. He would come back with a four-wheeler and chainsaw. As a logger, he would cut a path to drive in. He would quarter the moose and take it out, making four trips.

We never got a moose. We had a great time. Brevity requires that I save the rest of the moose hunting stories for some later writing project. Even with two experienced hunters, I had yet to solve my problem of finding suitable hunting companions. That moose hunting trip was never repeated.

Now the Ontario government will sell non-resident licenses only through registered guide services. As an American you can only hunt moose in Canada if you hire one of these guide services. You do everything as a package deal—hotel, meals, guide services, and license. Sorry, I won't play that game.

Both DeVor and Leach passed from this life in 2010. Dick DeVor was 66. Jim Leach was 92. The foundry on campus where Jim Leach taught was bulldozed to build some high-tech shrine. Dick DeVor now has a laboratory named in his honor. Dick DeVor and I parted ways. My memories of Jim Leach are something I cherish. They broke the mold after making him.

Mechanical Engineering: Revisited

MY CAREER CHOICE was cast into place during the spring of 1957. While a senior in high school, I set my sights on becoming a car designer. The next step in the logic directed me to enroll in college in engineering—notably mechanical engineering. To compound matters, I proceeded to earn three degrees in mechanical engineering. In 1968 at age 29, I opted to pursue a career in academia teaching mechanical engineering. I accepted a position as Assistant Professor at the University of Illinois. Academia helped to shield me from my decision to pursue a career in mechanical engineering. I was able to focus on mathematical and esoteric elegance. I was far enough up the food chain that I didn't get bogged down with the common nitty-gritty of mechanical engineering.

In my entire span of working years, I was able, in most cases, to avoid employment as a run-of-the-mill mechanical engineer. Upon reflection, I believe being a mechanical engineer is a life of servitude. The practicing mechanical engineer constantly has his or her nose in reference sources, sources that provide answers and standards. Typical reference sources include *Mark's Mechanical Engineering Handbook, The C.R.C. Math Tables,* and the classic standard *Shigley's Mechanical Design.*

Yes, I consulted at times and took on summer positions in

industry, but I tended to not be engaged performing actual engineering work. Most of my industrial experiences focused on performing autopsies of failed preexisting project designs. I was hired to tell companies why someone else's design had failed. The goal was to help the respective companies avoid repeating whatever design or conceptual errors had been made.

Dumb Dickie's Encounter with 9/11

IN THE LATE FALL OF 1975, I was contacted by structural engineers involved with the World Trade Center Twin Towers. Mr. Fred Chang, Professional Engineer, had become aware of my published work on stabilization of tall structures. Chang had encountered a wind sway problem and was seeking answers to help solve his problem. I told him I would be traveling east over the Christmas break. We scheduled a visit and firsthand look.

On Tuesday, December 23, 1975, I arrived at Chang's office in New York City. After discussing Chang's problem, I was not able to be of much help. The visit was cordial. I learned many things, things that I had previously only been able to speculate about.

Because of my keen interest in structural sway stabilization practices, I requested a tour of the WTC Twin Towers. I wanted to see the much acclaimed 3M dampers that had been retrofitted into the towers to address wind sway issues. Together, a small group of us ascended to the 82nd floor of the South Tower. Interior work was still being done. I got to inspect several 3M dampers in place on the exposed structural beams.

To my amazement, my eye caught a sight that disturbed me greatly.

The steel structural beams and the steel overhead ceiling

trusses were naked—devoid of the customary heat protective insulation. I was aware that insulation on structural steel members was mandated by building codes, fire safety inspectors, and accepted practices.

Upon raising my concerns with the structural engineers, Fred Chang gave me answers. I wasn't pleased with his answers, but nonetheless here is a summary of what Chang said. A building code waiver had been requested and granted. The WTC Twin Towers were thus exempted from prevailing practices.

Chang then cited five justifications for the waiver:
- The WTC Twin Towers were equipped with sprinkler systems.
- There was an early detection system in place, thus any fire would be identified quickly and by zone.
- Combustibles were maintained at low levels.
- Fire fighters would respond quickly.
- Any fire would be confined to a localized area of the building.

Although I was highly skeptical of the absence of insulation, I had few means to object or refute Chang's position.

History now confirms that both Twin Towers were struck by commandeered airliners on September 11, 2001. Both towers subsequently collapsed. The death toll exceeded 2,700, including 343 fire fighters and 71 police officers.

I submit that the WTC Twin Towers were poised to fall given provocation. Had proper insulation been in place, the outcome on 9/11 would have been quite different.

Of course, other theories abound. Theories are called theories because that's all they are—just theories. However, validation of my claim of no insulation is easy to establish.

The above photograph by Andrea Booher/FEMA News shows World Trade Center beam debris. Permission to reproduce is greatly appreciated and acknowledged.

If insulation had been applied and in place on the supporting steel beams, the insulation would be evident to some extent in the wreckage. There was no insulation—none at all.

In my book, *The Deadly Gamble*, I tell this story in much greater detail.

The Amateur vs. the Professional

IN THE SUMMER OF 1976, Marjorie and I moved to a hobby farm we had purchased in Champaign County. We acquired forty acres with a ranch-style home, a large barn previously used for horses, and a small pond for sport and fishing.

Due in large part to the urging of Marjorie's father, we soon had seven heifers to grow into stock cows. The idea was to let the stock cows produce calves and keep the grassy fields eaten. That would solve or at least lessen my mowing responsibilities.

The heifers were largely Angus with some Simmental and Holstein mixed in. I arranged for a local farmer, a neighbor, to haul the heifers from my father-in-law's farm in eastern Iowa to our farm in Dewey, Illinois. They arrived in the fall of 1976. My father-in-law had both beef and dairy cows. He and I decided to transport heifers as they, being young, would make the transition better than adult cows. I settled up with him and now owned seven heifers.

The problem was that one of them had been naughty. She had dated too young. Of course, there may have been a naughty bull involved, too. By the spring of 1977, it was obvious she was about to calf. When we had selected the heifers, we didn't realize that one of them had already been bred. Because I am formal and like to introduce everybody, this heifer's name was Goldie. As the name suggests, Goldie was lighter in color than the other six heifers, due to the Simmental in her breeding.

Because Goldie was due to calf, I had taken the precaution of having her penned up in what had been a horse stall. The stall was small as horse stalls normally go. It was 10' by 10'. The size was irrelevant, but I like to be accurate.

One Sunday morning, Marjorie, Vicki, and I got in the car to go to church. On the way past the barn, I stopped and quickly went in to check on Goldie. That was when I noticed a calf's hoof starting to protrude. We went on to church, expecting to come home and find a calf suckling on the new mother.

Upon my return, I again stopped in the drive. Alas, there had been no progress. It was at that point that I knew I had a problem.

The gist of the problem was obvious—the calf had only one leg ready to come out. Normally, the birthing happens with both front legs together. The fact that one leg was bent back and not in the normal birthing position prevented the calf from coming out.

I had never faced this problem before. Farming was new to me. I had never been involved in calving, much less a calving with calf positioning problems.

I made two telephone calls. The first was to a neighbor, the same one who had hauled the heifers from Iowa. His wife, Beverly, was familiar with the problem. Beverly kindly came to my farm. I also telephoned my father-in-law in Iowa. Dad Maxwell gave me the basics of what to do.

The basics were simple. Merely, push the protruding leg back in. Then reach in and grab the other leg, the one bent backwards. The idea was to push the calf back in sufficiently such that the calf's position was corrected.

I did that, or tried to, for better than an hour. Unfortunately, each time the bent leg got straightened out and in position, the formerly straight leg took the place of the bent leg. After about 1

½ hours, I was exhausted and no closer to getting the calf birthed.

I went to the house and telephoned a veterinarian.

Doc Cline (no relation) arrived. He first examined the heifer, Goldie. Doc then got out some chains that resembled choke chains used on aggressive dogs. Each chain had a ring on the end. Doc applied some lubricant to his working hand and arm. He went in and attached the chain to a leg, by using the chain pushed back through the ring. Doc Cline did all this attaching while his hand was deep within the heifer. Then he did the same thing to the second front leg.

Then Doc Cline caught me by surprise. He got out a third chain and went in one more time. Now, Doc had three chains in his hands. I don't remember if he used a calf puller, but let's grant that as an affirmative.

Within five minutes after his initial examination, the calf was out and on the straw in the stall. Doc Cline had used the third chain on the calf's head. The three chains allowed Doc to control both front legs and the calf's head.

Sadly, the calf was born dead, but at least Goldie was saved.

Doc gave the heifer an injection. Then he got his chains and gear washed, cleaned up, and returned to his truck. As Doc prepared to leave after washing his hands, I looked at him and asked a philosophical question. "I am big and strong. I had advice from the best experts I could find. How is it that I tried for 1 ½ hours and failed, but you came and had the calf out in five minutes?"

Doc calmly replied, "I have studied the rule book; I am familiar with the basic moves; I have played the game before."

To that I will add a fourth reason: Doc Cline came suited up and carrying the right equipment.

I have come to deeply respect professionals. The amateur has little chance playing against the professional. I found it to be significant that Doc Cline didn't use advanced or intricate moves. Instead, he had used basic moves.

My mistake in this calf-birthing saga was in not realizing that I was over my head. By the time I messed around and failed, the calf was dead. Or maybe it was dead before I even started. I guess we'll never know for sure. For completeness, I will add that it was a bull calf and by most standards, it was also large. Goldie, as a heifer, was just 18 months old at the time. She had not yet reached her full maturity. Despite this poor beginning, Goldie went on to produce a string of calves during her tenure.

Cows are like people—they have distinct personalities. Goldie's personality modelled that of my mother. She held her head up in the air, kept a distance from me, and was a fence-jumper. When I finally gave up being in the cow business, I took great delight in loading up Goldie to go to the sale barn. I regretted selling some of my other cows, but not Goldie!

The UAW Played a Joke on Me

FOR MY FIRST 24 YEARS of car ownership, I only drove used cars. Being mechanically adept, I was reasonably successful in keeping my older cars running. At age 40, I splurged and purchased my first new car, a 1979 Ford LTD station wagon. I asked the dealer to add a towing package. The dealer came back saying that the car was already equipped with a towing package. The car had the beefier C-6 Ford transmission and the extra heat exchanger to cool the transmission fluid. I encountered one problem: the starter's Bendix gear commonly failed to engage. After a year or two of struggle, I determined the source of the problem. A simple pin had been left out during the assembly of the starter's Bendix engagement mechanism.

In 1982 I took on a summer position with Hughes Aircraft Company in southern California. While driving in the desert heat, my idiot light indicated an overheated engine.

I feel compelled to expound on what is called an idiot light— and how Ford's decision to replace gauges with idiot lights impacted me. In the days of my youth, virtually all cars had five gauges on the dashboard. These were: speedometer; fuel; voltage (in the electrical system); engine temperature; and lastly oil pressure. Car designers and manufacturers started making cars without all those gauges. Costs were reduced and they reasoned that many drivers either never looked at the gauges or possibly were not able to discern any useful information from them. A simple binary or on-off light would illuminate indicating a problem, such as an overheating engine.

My 1979 Ford LTD had an idiot light and no temperature gauge. Astute drivers disliked such lights, and thus commonly referred to them as idiot lights: something useful for idiots. My Ford LTD's idiot light must have had a high threshold for triggering. I drove a car with an overheating engine for three years before I became aware of any problem. The light finally came on in the summer of 1982 as I drove across the intensely hot Mojave Desert, on my way to Palm Springs from Los Angeles. My engine was getting fried and I never even knew it—much less the why.

For the sake of brevity, I will merely state that over a 12-year span from 1979 to 1991, I went through two engines and three transmissions. I usually assumed that I was dealing with a bad thermostat, or possibly a water pump with defective impeller blades, or even a foreign object like a shop rag or a tennis ball somewhere within the car's cooling system.

In 1991, I finally decided to pull the radiator to have it flushed out and professionally serviced. The old guy in the radiator shop took one look and then made a pronouncement: the car had the wrong radiator. My engine was the larger 351 cubic-inch Windsor Ford engine and not the normal 302 cubic-inch Ford engine. It seems that when the LTD was built at a Ford assembly plant in Ohio in 1979, the wrong radiator had been installed. The LTD had only a 2-core radiator, whereas the Windsor engine required a thicker 3-core radiator.

It became obvious to me that a disgruntled United Auto Workers (UAW) line employee had sabotaged my car on the assembly line. It was his joke—but I didn't laugh. This type of sabotage was fairly common as union factory workers were unhappy with their Ford contract.

I had no way of detecting the wrong radiator, so I had just struggled with overheating for years with no clear explanation.

One of my Dumb Dickie mistakes was in hiring a shop to install a new engine, but not replacing the radiator at the same time.

Ford Motor Company's union problems have been largely resolved. I remain to this day unsympathetic to the plight of the day-to-day union worker. An act of sabotage against a paying customer stands as a sin of commission. I label the sabotage as a deliberate act. In 1979 computers were sufficiently advanced and used to identify each vehicle frame and description as the vehicle underwent assembly. A computer-generated sheet clearly specified the thicker radiator. Surely, other means existed for the UAW to resolve its contract differences with Ford. As an idealistic person, I feel that the UAW owes me a letter of apology. Obviously, that letter will never come.

My dumbness was exceptional considering I was trained in mechanical engineering. As the years of dealing with overheating slipped by, I was too dumb to crack the problem. In life we often make assumptions—assumptions that cost us. I fought overheating problems for 12 years. By then my car had been relegated to junk status. I was so disgusted with the Ford LTD wagon that I fantasized hiring a junkyard to compress the car into a cubicle. I imagined something like the scene in *Goldfinger,* where the bad guys compress a Lincoln convertible into a cube the size of a coffee table. Imagining its destruction once and for all was the most satisfaction I could get out of the car at that point.

"Huh? What's That You Say?"

I STARTED WORKING in and otherwise being exposed to loud environments in 1966. I had taken a summer job at Corning Glass Works. With some extra cash I started to take private pilot lessons. For the next two decades I logged several thousand hours flying in noisy airplanes. It wasn't until many years into flying that I realized the importance of proper hearing protection.

In the early 1970s I acquired a Remington chainsaw. I did all sorts of tree removal for my father-in-law. In 1976, Marjorie and I moved to a forty-acre hobby farm in Champaign County, Illinois. I mowed a large yard. I also cut and baled hay for stock cows. The machinery was noisy.

In the summer of 1982, I was employed at Hughes Aircraft. A routine employment examination by doctors revealed that I was suffering considerable hearing loss, especially in my right ear. I was 43 years young at the time. It was a serious error in my life to be engaged in noisy environments while failing to wear proper hearing protection.

The World's Second Best Salesman

IN THE SUMMER OF 1981, I took on a consulting job near Boston. I was hired to perform an autopsy—to tell a company why their product wasn't functioning properly. I was paid well. I desperately needed the income to keep my other business investments solvent. That story will come. This story concerns my encounter with the world's second best salesman.

I needed to buy a suit. Marjorie and I went to a clothing store. I looked at suits. Nothing met my fancy.

Then I made a terrible error: I explained to the young salesman why I was leaving without buying a suit. The suits I had looked at were silver, gray, blue, and black but my wardrobe was based on earth colors like browns, tans, and greens.

That was my undoing.

The salesman remarked that earth colors are great for young people. He pointed out that I had aged, my hair had silvered in color. As a distinguished mature man, he suggested it was time for me to adopt a new standard in my wardrobe that accented the tones in my distinguished silver hair.

I ended up purchasing not one, but two suits that day.

When dealing with a salesperson, never tell the salesperson why you are rejecting his or her products. Once you make that error, you open the door for the salesperson to counter your thinking. In addition to two suits, I went out the door with matching ties and accessories. I still wear these suits. I actually wear them often.

I have a side joke about suits and weddings. I keep suits a long time. When I attend a wedding, I can usually say that my suit is older than the bride. Few brides in today's world were born prior to 1981. There are some, of course, but I still claim that I am correct in saying few.

You'll notice that I referred to the salesperson as the second best in the world. I reserve the #1 title for Alexander Botts. Botts was a fictional character in a book I highly recommend: *The Fabulous Saga of Alexander Botts and The Earthworm Tractor.*

LIFE GOES ON

Dumb Dickie Learns from His Mistakes,
While Still Making New Ones
(1978-1998)

Going into Business with Relatives

MY DUMB MISTAKES continued as I grew to adulthood, including possibly the two dumbest things I have ever done in my lifetime.

The first was to agree to enter into a business relationship with my wife's family members, specifically my sister-in-law and her husband. In 1978, I had the opportunity to purchase a 20-unit apartment complex in Naples, Florida. Being stupid and in need of additional investors, four people made the purchase of what was then called Gulf Winds Motel Apartments. The four people were my wife Marjorie, her younger sister, her sister's husband, and yours truly. I had gone into business with relatives. That turned out to be an incredible blunder on my part.

We owned the property for four years. Management of a rental property from a distance of a thousand miles was challenging. We made incredible returns on our investment on paper, but the cash flow was immensely negative. In short, as investors we were under-capitalized. Property values escalated. Within four years the property purchased for $525,000 was sold on paper for about $1.3M. The problem was that money on paper isn't money.

All three of my partners didn't want a cash sale but rather insisted on getting a higher price, but where the higher price was in paper. This means that when we sold we became holders of contractual property notes or simply "paper." Paper notes are only good so long as the notes are in fact honored. Additionally, my three partners didn't want to pay the capital gains tax. This caused us to enter into a Section 1031 tax-free exchange. We exchanged our Florida real estate equity position for about 500 acres of farm land in Iowa. Land values in Iowa had escalated dramatically in the late 1970s and early 1980s, so the farmland in Iowa *circa* 1982 was valued at about $3,600 per acre.

Almost within minutes of that tax-free exchange in 1982, the value of Midwestern farm land plummeted. Land values dropped to a low of about $800 per acre. Commodity prices fell as well. The problem was made worse because the land contract involved substantial debt obligations. This debt service required us to pay interest at 6% on about $3,000 of debt per acre. The debt servicing obligation alone was about $180 per acre. Because of the collapse in commodity prices, primarily corn and soybeans, the landlord's share of the crop didn't come close to meeting the contracted debt servicing. We also had to pay property taxes and our share of seed, herbicides, and fertilizer, etc.

There was no way I could handle the debt service and negative cash flow. We had vastly over-leveraged our position. Leverage works great in an up market. It is a killer in a down market. Then the Florida promissory notes went into default. It was like a stake had been driven through our hearts. The buyers in Florida had attempted some sort of condominium timeshare that went belly-up. This coincided with the overall real estate collapse in the early 1980s. Recall that Jimmy Carter's runaway inflation hit the skids as Ronald Reagan instituted vastly different economic policies. The economic apple tree was being shaken violently. My leveraged position was untenable.

An accountant in Florida had a reflective comment, "Bears make money and bulls make money, but pigs go to slaughter." By leveraging we were acting as bulls, but the bull must be able to get out when the market reverses. The refusal of bull investors to recognize the bear market makes them pigs. Pigs want it both ways. Again, pigs go to slaughter.

The inability of my partners to accept that the market had reversed caused them to freeze and become paralyzed. They did nothing. Over a few years, I lost money at a hemorrhaging rate, at about $1 per minute for three years. Moreover, I was powerless to stop the bleeding because my three partners voted, at every turn, against me.

All this time I was meeting periodically with my banker as I had to renew or "roll over" notes to provide cash flow for things like seed purchases and other crop expenses. My banker knew exactly what I was doing and approved. Now think of this: If you go to Las Vegas and shoot craps, yes, you can lose $2M easily. Few bankers would lend you money for such investment strategies. On the reverse side, try to envision how near-to-impossible it would be for you to lose $2M while making only the moves that were approved by your banker.

Upon reflection, in 1982 my partners and I could have sold the Florida holdings for, say, $850K in cash. That is exactly the position I had advocated. We would have made about $300K in gains in four short years. That wasn't good enough for my partners. Instead my partners, behaving as pigs, insisted on the pie in the sky of selling at $1.3M and also on not paying any capital gains tax.

I want to comment on the investment in Naples, Florida, from the standpoint of return on investment. The purchase price in 1978 was $525,000, but our initial outlay in hard money was only about $50,000. The rest of the contract price was carried in loan obligations. If we had sold for cash in 1982 for, say, $850,000, we would have walked away with gains of about $300,000 in cash. Leverage works fantastically in an inflationary market. With Jimmy Carter's inept economic policies, inflation was the hallmark of his presidency. Commercial loan interest rates got to be so high that I can recall renewing one bank loan at 22% per annum interest. The opportunity to walk away with $300K from an initial investment of $50,000 was something people can only dream about, either then or now. Unfortunately, pigs are pigs and that is why pigs go to slaughter.

My partners accepted the good times easily, but when the markets reversed, they refused to agree to liquidation. I went from having a personal net worth of about $2M to waking up one day about $800K in debt. I had lost close to $3M—and had no way to stop the hemorrhaging of my position. All land and contract purchases had been in my personal name. I realized too late the gravity of failing to operate under benefit of corporate veil. Because I was personally liable, each and every asset in my name was at risk. At each attempt to extract myself I was faced with a 3-to-1 vote against me. It seems that Marjorie had a genetic defect in that she would always vote with her sister—and against me.

In 1984 as my position worsened, I met with an attorney in Danville, Illinois for the purpose of filing bankruptcy. The attorney agreed that I was bankrupt and had only the last step to take: actually filing for bankruptcy. As a last-ditch effort, with frustration mounting and hope vanishing, I decided to take matters into my own hands before declaring bankruptcy. My debt was owed to holders of contract deeds. Five different parties or individuals were in some way involved in the contract chain for the primary property, a 331-acre farm in Floyd County, Iowa. Moreover, all five parties in the contract chain were at considerable risk. If the first domino fell, that being me, then each of the successive contract parties going back up the chain would fall in turn.

Over a period of ten days starting in March of 1985, I wrote three letters to all of the people involved in the contract chain. My objectives were to educate the recipients about certain realities and for me to gain control of the situation. This was the

1985 version of my ham-through-windshield predicament. I set out once again to gain control of a chaotic situation.

As an educator, my task was clear. I had to educate the people in the contract chain. The first party was a family of three siblings who had inherited the 331 acres in Floyd County. The family's name was Seaton. The Seatons were all older. The unmarried brother worked for the post office somewhere. The two sisters were both spinsters. I was dealing with people who had little taste for a fight—these siblings had inherited the land, as opposed to working for it.

Because both my brother-in-law and I had the title "Doctor" in front of our names, the Seaton siblings assumed they could squeeze us and magically get money. I made the following picture clear in my three letters.

My partners and I had no assets and no ability to pay. At that time we were in arrears on making the required contractual annual payment.

I was asking that we deed the property back to the heirs and let everybody walk away—to move on with our respective lives.

Should the heirs not accept my suggestion, then I would use the lawful weapons at my disposal to attack them.

My first weapon was that I still had possession of the land. I stated my intention to discharge the tenant and to take over farming the land myself. I had one tractor and a few basic implements. I would feebly attempt farming, but obviously would do poorly. In the three years that the legal system would take for them to regain possession, three things would happen: 1) They would receive no income or payments; 2) Production would drop, causing the USDA production base on the farm to drop. Government crop subsidies were determined by past production, which would diminish during the three years of my projected control; and 3) Because of my poor farming practices, the weeds would get out of control.

My next weapon would be to cause the heirs and the others

in the contract chain to be publicly shamed and ridiculed. The farm was located on a state highway, Route 218. I would go out onto the highway and make a public spectacle of myself. In order to get noticed, I would wear a barrel, similar to what the ultra down-and-out did in the Great Depression. Traffic would slow and even stop to see what was happening. I would pass out news fliers and give press interviews. I also claimed I would erect Burma-Shave style signs along the highway, with rhyming slogans telling the world of my unfair treatment. I would point out how unreasonable all parties had been in the contract chain.

As an added touch, I made it clear in my letters that I was insane. I told my readers of how God had punished those before them who had insulted me or otherwise done me harm. I told the story of Murphy's death in a head-on collision. I went on to tell of others who had perished after doing me harm. Yes, sadly, as many as a dozen people have died in violent situations, usually within three months of doing harm to me. Murphy, who as you recall sold me a junk engine, was the first. Oddly, two others named Murphy also died in head-on collisions. I had purchased a Ford station wagon from Bob Murphy Ford in Morton, Illinois. The car had been previously driven by Murphy's wife. It turned out to be a lemon, with bad valves. Bob Murphy died after that in a head-on collision. Stranger still, Bob Murphy's wife died in a head-on collision after her husband. The locals in Morton marveled as how strange it was that both husband and wife died in separate head-on collisions. If only they knew. I could recount another ten violent deaths, but I have made my point. God will punish any and all who attempt to harm me. I have also made my point that I am insane, and you should keep a long distance from me if evil is your intention.

I show below the newspaper photograph. I had gained enough public attention to be invited to speak to an audience at the Linn County Fair in Marion, Iowa, in September 1985. The farm economy was in a tailspin, so the topic of my financial plight was shared with a farm audience. Yes, I was interviewed by the press.

Below is an excerpt from my journal, illustrating dramatically another punishment that God inflicted on one of my foes.

4/6/1985, Page 118, Volume 3

We are now in Iowa visiting Marjorie's parents. An interesting occurrence involved Attorney Robert Todd of Muscatine, Iowa. Todd represented my former, but now estranged, partners. As their attorney, Todd maintained a strict policy of having no contact with me, interacting only through my attorney, Tom Gordon. Of course, Todd couldn't stop me from sending my letters. My letters to Todd, being sent First

Class, were presumably delivered as none ever came back
marked as "refused." It would be fair to say that Todd and I were
adversarial. Clearly, Attorney Robert Todd was not a champion
of R.E. Klein. In fact, I never met or even spoke on the
telephone with him.

It seems that Todd's house burned to the ground. He came
home one day and found a hole in the ground where his house
used to be. The fire trucks were just leaving as he arrived. You
have to appreciate that this event occurred within just a few days
following Todd having received Klein letter number two. In
that letter, filled with fire and brimstone, I ranted on about God
having a history of favoring me over my adversaries.

All parties in the contract chain had to agree and sign off on
the contract's termination. That included my now estranged
sister-in-law and her husband.

Assuming that I went into default on the contract, meaning
making no payments, litigation against me would require several
years for starters. Then, as that window would close, I would
seek bankruptcy protection, thus adding more delay. All during
this time, I could still maintain control of the farmland. In that
time as a stall strategy, the farmland would have been farmed
poorly—by me personally. So I am a poor farmer, that isn't a
crime. My primary weapon boiled down to the threat that I
would farm the land myself and would obviously do a poor job.
After multiple years of litigation, my creditors would get
nothing and also get back weed-infested unproductive farmland.
Moreover, its federal agricultural basis on which the government
farm subsidy payments hinged would have been degraded.

In my three letters I made these points vividly clear. Within a
few weeks the creditors and all parties in the contract chain
agreed. The writing of those three letters effectively saved me
from being $800K in debt and eliminated my negative cash flow
situation. It also prevented me from having to declare

bankruptcy.

In rough terms, each letter pushed away a quarter of a million dollars in debt. That's a pretty outstanding return for composing each of the three letters.

The reality was that all five parties were at considerable risk if some sort of resolution didn't materialize. The key to the problem's solution was to cause the original holders of the Floyd County farm to accept it back and to cancel all debts in exchange, except for a small payment of $11,000 by each of the other four parties in the contract chain. Yes, I paid the $11,000, but in doing so I was relieved of about $800K in debt obligations. My actions got me out of the fire, and in the process, it got four other additional parties in the contract chain out of the fire as well.

Even to this day I have not received a single thanks. Deep in my files I still have copies of those three letters. At some point I will hopefully make them available. It isn't common that one is able to reap $800K in benefits merely by writing three letters.

I am reminded of a quotation by Robert A. Heinlein, the science fiction writer (roughly paraphrased): "The poor bloke who is in debt $800 has to tighten his belt; whereas the bloke who owes $800K will never miss a meal."

Heinlein's point was that when debts become massive, they will never be paid off. As a consequence, the world will leave the bloke alone. In my letters my main objective was to inform the original deed holders that they could cry all they wanted and make whatever demands they wanted, but you can't get money if it isn't there. The Seatons opted to enter into a big-stakes game of speculating on the dollar's weakness. They, like many others, came up short. The best thing for them to do was to pick up the pieces and move on. My proposition was that they would be vastly better off by merely taking the farm back and letting me walk away. They soon realized it was in their best interests to do exactly that. My three letters accomplished that objective.

Again, with the benefit of hindsight, the tax-free exchange of the Florida property for Iowa farmland has to be viewed as a colossally dumb move. Almost instantly after acquiring the Iowa farmland its market value plummeted. In contrast, the Gulf Winds property, as ocean frontage property, became pivotal in a later real estate move. That parcel was the key land tract in permitting a large hotel chain to bulldoze it level and build in its place a multi-acre high rise modern hotel. That Naples property became worth many millions of dollars because it was the critical piece of a much larger real estate manipulation.

I was able to get my life back in order. I always like to think of David who feigned insanity by drooling and scratching the wall (I Samuel 21:13). The ability to feign insanity can be a valuable asset and lifesaver at times.

Following are two journal excerpts in which I express my exultation at the conclusion of this episode in my life, and my attitude about having tackled my problems rather than giving up.

***

8/8/1985, Page 181, Volume 3

Attorney Tom Gordon and I talked about the various Klein letters and the sagging farm situation. Tom indicated that if I had approached him today with the same problem, a similar solution would be hopeless. The national farm economy has now sagged so deep that we should be elated that we are out of it. In retrospect, being successful was due to my keen mind and Tom's skill as a negotiator, plus the fact that neither he nor I ever quit.

It was a most rewarding conversation and appraisal of the situation. Instead of running like a scared dog, tail between its legs and dropping everything, I am now in a situation where time is on my side and my downside risk is non-existent. R.E. Klein—by training, temperament, skill, and tenacity—will attack slowly and methodically, like a starfish using its tentacles (five arms) to keep continual pressure on the victim, the clam. The clam, although stronger, is ultimately defeated by the starfish, because the starfish can alter muscles and allow three arms out of five to rest, whereas the clam cannot relax its single strong muscle.

Klein will thrive on the attack itself. The process of attacking an evil foe is like a liquor which intoxicates.

These past 3 to 4 weeks are, to date, the high point of my life. It seems that virtually all of my adversaries are on the run. It is an exhilarating experience. The feeling of victory and accomplishment is within me. As I become overwhelmed with the activities of the past 1 ½ months, it seems that I am ready to burst, so to speak. My mind keeps running at a frantic pace such that I can't stop it even if I try. If I try to rest, to listen to the radio, or even mow the lawn, I can't get my mind to stop tossing all of the items up in the air for view. During the 4 days it took to compose my third letter, my mind viewed and tossed it over and over again. My brain keeps popping like a kettle of popcorn over a stove.

9/6/1985, Page 212, Volume 3

Murray Wise and I visited over the phone today. He told me a story about the relationship between agriculture and the recent Japan Airline Flight 123 which crashed on August 12, 1985. The airliner, a Boeing 747, lost its tail section due to improper installation. Without its tail section, the airliner also lost all hydraulic systems. Even the wing ailerons were inoperative. With power the airliner maintained flight, but had no maneuverability and impacted a mountain. All 521 passengers and crew on board knew that a crash was inevitable. Given 30 to 40 minutes to live, it is worthy to note what the passengers and crew did on board. The passengers divided themselves into three distinct groups. Those in the rear section devoted their time to prayer. Those seated elsewhere wanting to join the prayer group relocated to the rear. Another group chose to sit in the midsection and write letters to family and loved ones, in the hope that their notes would survive the crash. The third group chose to enjoy an open bar and proceeded to have a good time. This group of party-goers moved forward to be closer to the bar area. The people thus chose to spend their 30 minutes or so by either praying, communicating to others, or having a good time. Murray implied that this was symbolic of agriculture today. Agriculture as we know it is on a final glide, in an uncontrolled fashion, to its death. Those on board don't have many options.

I will make some remarks on the symbolism of the Japan Airliner crash. I argue that the passengers did have some means of control. The Boeing 747 had over 500 people on board. Any shift or movement of those people would result in a change in what is called trim. The airliner could, in theory, have banked, thus allowing for yaw or directional control. Moreover, the passengers could have shifted their weight fore to aft. The combination of an aft shift and reduced power would cause a slow descent. I assert that a slow descent to a water landing would be preferable to broadsiding a mountain.

In sum, the trim of an aircraft can be influenced by center of gravity changes. By moving about within the cabin area in an organized manner, the flight could have been controlled and thus manipulated. That would have required two things: knowledge of what to do and leadership to cause it to happen.

My qualifications are simple, three in particular: a doctorate in mechanical engineering, specialization in control systems, and qualification as an instrument-rated pilot.

The 747 is symbolic of my life and farm crisis struggle. I recall my first meeting with Murray Wise where I first discussed my farm crash in late 1983 or early 1984. I know we discussed how to best approach Seaton et al. Attorney Knashaug had advised me to just file my bankruptcy petition with the court, believing my situation as hopeless. But I wasn't willing to go down without a fight. That triggered my move to engage an attorney willing to fight. Attorney Tom Gordon and I worked well as a team and were ultimately successful.

R.E. Klein vs. the State of Iowa

THROUGHOUT MY FINANCIAL CRISIS involving Iowa farmland, another battle came forth. The Iowa Department of Revenue started to hound me with threatening letters. Their records showed that I had received $29,000 in federal farm subsidies for one year. They couldn't find my Iowa non-resident tax return. Iowa tax law required me to file an Iowa tax return if my net Iowa-based income exceeded $600 in any tax year. Yes, I received $29K in federal farm subsidy payments, but I also paid out more than that in interest, crop expenses, hail insurance, and property taxes. My federal Schedule F for the Floyd County farm showed a negative number, therefore I was exempt from filing an Iowa income tax return. The lady sending me threatening letters demanded that I send her my Federal Form 1040 to prove my lack of net income.

The Federal Form 1040 is a private matter between the federal government and the taxpayer. I refused her request. Yes, she could file tax charges against me, but she had nothing concrete to base her charges on, except for the $29K. She lacked anything to go on so long as she didn't have my federal tax return or any returns I had filed.

I knew a fundamental fact. If I provided my Federal 1040 with schedules, the State of Iowa would file a state income tax return on my behalf. Once the state return existed, Iowa would next demand an audit. That would involve trips, accountancy fees, and my time.

The State of Iowa had the option to file criminal charges against me for failure to file a non-resident tax return. That would be a high bar for them to attempt. Iowa had a suspicion, but no solid proof of my alleged failure to file a return.

My eventual move was to send the Iowa tax lady a letter declaring my federal return as private. I did inform her that the land contract records in Iowa counties, including Floyd County, were public. She could go there to see that I indeed was obligated to pay far more in interest on my contract than the farm received in income, including the federal crop subsidies of $29,000.

I was amused with the threatening tone in her letters. One letter had the words FINAL NOTICE typed across the top. That letter had been sent to me using Certified Mail. Because it was my "final notice," I laughed to myself that I would never hear from her again. After sending my above mentioned letter, I never heard from Ms. Merilee Magg again.

N8478W, the Final Cross-Country

I'VE TOLD MANY STORIES that included my flying club's workhorse, Piper Cherokee PA-28-180, N8478W.

This story took place in the fall of 1982. The month was most likely November. One member of the club was flying in the western part of New Jersey. The land was rolling and somewhat wooded. It was after dark. A friend of the club member was at the controls. An experienced pilot with extensive instrument flying, the man manipulating the controls was attempting what turned out to be a tragic mistake: He was trying to land at an unlighted grass strip. I was later told that he had lived in the area. He felt comfortable using neighborhood house and street lights to guide him in for landing. It's great to be a hero and do it if you can, but it's stupidity galore when you mess up. The pilot miscalculated, landing at flight speed with most of the runway behind him. Landing that far down the runway, he was out of both options and runway. N8478W careened, striking an embankment at the runway's end. N8478W had become a retractable. The two main wheels were gone. Fortunately, nobody was injured. There was no fire.

The following day, N8478W was dragged, possibly by a tow truck using portable wheel dollies, to a place of dishonor.

The owner of the airfield was livid, as the sanctity of his airstrip had been violated. I assumed that locals had been calling for the closure of the field. The word "angry" would be an understatement.

The flying club, with its 20 shareholders/members had to decide what to do. The members were mostly university types, commonly professors with doctorates. The member who had allowed his pilot friend to fly and crash was Sid. I don't know Sid's real name. He was a doctoral student in aeronautical engineering. Sid was from India. He spoke a rapid-fire English with a penetrating voice, almost a shrill. Sid was small in stature, but his shrill voice was overpowering. In addition, he wasn't shy about telling you how to solve each and every problem in life. Sid was quick on the draw—with his mouth.

The club's maintenance officer was Dr. Fred Brown, a full professor of physics. Fred was also opinionated and unabashed. I would describe Fred Brown as a Nervous Nellie. Fred worried about all sorts of little things. Everything had to be just right. Fred had his opinions and wasn't shy about voicing them. Other people's opinions were of no value to him. Fred was way short on compromise.

The club argued about to what to do. Sell the wreckage on

the spot? Haul it back home and salvage good parts, notably the electronics and the engine that had just undergone an expensive overhaul? Some argued that the damage was slight and that the airplane should be repaired. Some wanted the aircraft brought back so we could have our local aircraft mechanics inspect it. The critical question concerned the integrity of the internal structural members in the wings. Did the wheel assembly get bent, or did the impact damage the wings' internal structural members?

At the time, I believe I was also the club's president. As the bickering went on, I finally declared that I would drive my truck to New Jersey to bring N8478W back to Illinois. My faithful friend Jim Leach had a tandem flatbed trailer available for my use. I was set to go east. As was my custom when I would be out, I gave my students their exam in advance.

Sid said he would ride with me and assist. Fred Brown said he was going to be close to New Jersey and would join us. The three of us would load N8478W onto my trailer. We would then drive the carcass back to Illinois.

Please buckle your seat belts. Two professors and one squeaky Indian PhD student in aeronautical engineering would embark on this trip. The comedy is about to begin.

The trip east was okay, except for one problem. I was driving. Sid was in the passenger's seat. For countless hours, Sid blasted in my right ear a continual stream of gibberish. He talked about mathematics, stability theory, and who knows what else. We made it to Ohio—about halfway to New Jersey—when I asked Sid to stop talking and give my ears a rest. We arrived in New Jersey. I dropped Sid off at a hotel. I unhooked the trailer so I could take the truck to Connecticut for the night to see my parents.

The next morning, I returned to New Jersey, attached the trailer, and made my way to the airport.

Of course, Sid had somehow gotten a ride to the airport. He

had the airport owner stirred up worse than a hornets' nest. Fred arrived. My first problem was that the airport owner didn't like me. At first he didn't even allow me to drive onto his field. I explained that I had driven all the way from Illinois to retrieve the wrecked airplane. I said that if I couldn't drive onto the field now, I'd have to return some other time to get the wreckage removed. He initially refused to let me drive on his sod, as rains had recently softened the field. I finally got permission to back my trailer up to the wrecked airplane. I had to approach from the tail end. This was bad because most of the airplane's weight was concentrated in the engine, now at the rear of the trailer. Loading the plane that way made hauling unstable. A trailer with too much load to the rear will fishtail as speed increases. That is bad.

Nonetheless, I figured I would get the airplane onto the trailer and worry about weight management later. But I had a second problem. Airplanes don't fit well on highways. After the airplane was on the trailer, the wings had to be somehow removed. The day was cold and windy. My plan was to load and then move my truck and trailer to a place at the airport where I had some protection from the wind.

The airport owner finally softened as he and I interacted. My task was to convince him that I was up to the job. Sid had done me no favors. Fred Brown was of neutral value at this point. The airport owner was helpful in using jacks to lift the airplane. With my skill at backing up trailers, I soon had the trailer under N8478W and the airplane was lowered onto it.

I must add, my parents in Connecticut couldn't help but join in the action. They drove to New Jersey the day we loaded. My mother was helpful in calming down the airport owner. As I was backing up the trailer to go under N8478W, she remarked to the nervous man, "Don't underestimate him." Mother also brought with her some fresh-baked treats that we enjoyed on our long drive back to Illinois.

I drove the entire rig to a spot somewhat protected from the wind. The next task was the removal of the wings. Fred and Sid were so eager to do it that I wasn't able to get in the cockpit to take a look. For a while, Sid became all excited with his newest idea. He said, "We'll drill the bolts out!"

Sid's idea was preposterous to the point that I was in pain. Each wing was held in place by about eight or possibly ten hardened bolts. Moreover, these were long bolts, possibly six inches in length. Access to the bolt heads was difficult as the bolts were down inside the aircraft's thin sidewalls. The bolts passed through aluminum. A drill would never stay centered. We had only one old electric drill along and few decent drill bits. We were away from buildings, so access to electrical power would be a trick. To be successful drilling out the bolts, one must drill all sixteen or twenty bolts without a miss. Please note, I had few drill bits. Certainly I didn't have a drill bit long enough, much less the correct diameter. A single failed drilling attempt would have doomed the ability to remove the aircraft's wings. I hope I never fly in any airplane designed by Sid the Aeronautical Engineer. The man was a walking time-bomb.

It turned out that Fred and Sid spent several hours trying to loosen the hardened bolts inside the airplane's exterior side walls. Each wing was held by a row of vertical bolts.

The wings could be pulled out and away only if all bolts were removed. The heads of the bolts were difficult to reach. Sid and Fred were using vise-grip pliers, which only managed to mar the bolt heads and make the job harder. Again, I was dealing with two overly zealous nincompoops. They were both too stupid to realize they were stupid.

They didn't know tools or how to use them. And they didn't even know what tools I had along. I'd brought a wide array of tools as I didn't know what I would be up against.

After several hours of their monkeying around, I demanded to take a look. All this time I'd been standing out in the cold wind. As John Wayne said in the movie *The Cowboys,* "We're burning daylight."

Upon getting into the cockpit, I examined the bolts. From my awkward position, I determined which tools I needed and requested Fred hand them to me.

My request was simple.

"Hand me a 3/8ths ratchet, a 6-inch extension, and a 9/16ths swivel socket."

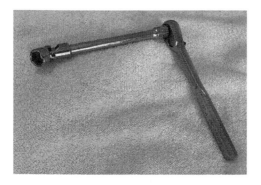

Fred looked in my toolbox. He handed me a 9/16ths combination wrench.

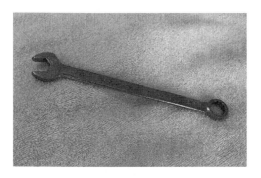

"Is this what you wanted?"

Bear in mind that Fred Brown was a full professor of physics. He had absolutely no clue what I was talking about. I climbed out of the cockpit and got the tools myself.

I had the bolts removed on both wings within about 20

minutes. Soon the wings were off and tucked lengthwise on each side of the trailer, leaning against the fuselage.

By now, it was late in the afternoon. I was chilled after being in the raw wind all day. And I still had to figure out what to do about the weight loading and trailer stability.

I made a decision. I would just pack, secure the load, and start driving. I assumed I could go 45MPH, which meant the trip would take about 20 hours. If I took the time to reload, somehow managing to swing the fuselage around, that would require us to stay overnight. I preferred to go slow and let the truck's engine work while I was in a warm cab.

By this point, Fred said he was riding with us. The three of us got into the truck. As we drove west, darkness was upon us. It was then that we discovered we had a wiring problem. The trailer lights were not working. Alongside the road, we tried to fix the lights. We needed to strip a wire to get a better connection. I went to get my wire strippers.

Sid excitedly proclaimed, "I do it with my teeth."

I did the job with my electrical wire stripper. This gives some clue as to how unhinged Sid was.

Because of exhaustion, we got hotel rooms in Pennsylvania for the night. The next morning, we set out early, with me determined to get home that same day.

At our slow speed, I wanted the most direct route. I wasn't going a mile farther than necessary. As we approached Indianapolis, I had to make a decision. I had travelled many times through Indy as opposed to around it on the beltway. I knew a shortcut on Indy's west side and took it, turning off the highway.

Fred just about went bonkers. He became so upset that he proclaimed, "I'm not responsible." Fred was visibly agitated, almost approaching hysterical.

Dear Fred, the reality was that I was driving my truck and I drove as I saw fit. And my shortcut did end up saving us time. I claim full responsibility.

About the trailer-towing instability, turns out that at 45MPH the trailer was stable. Upon getting up to 47 or 48 MPH, all would be well until I hit a pothole or other disturbance. The trailer would start fishtailing. The trick was in slowing down before the fishtailing became too violent. It was a fine line. The trip took the predicted 20 hours of driving time.

The club hosted a social event to say goodbye to N8478W. The club saved the engine, propeller, and radios. The carcass was sold to an aircraft salvage yard in central Illinois. Within a year, I stopped being an active pilot.

Fred Brown retired from the University of Illinois. He and his wife, Joan, moved to an island in Puget Sound. I read some years back that he passed away. I've lost track of Sid. I imagine he is still somewhere all excited, doing it with his teeth. If not that, he is drilling out hardened bolts.

Journalizing and Fountain Pens

MY LIFE IN THE EARLY 1980S was characterized by turmoil and upheaval. At times, it became difficult for me to grasp the stress I was under and figure out how to best cope. Two things literally changed my life.

The first thing was starting to write in a journal. I selected a journal from the student bookstore on campus. It had a sewn binding, numbered pages, and acid-free paper. Each journal was 300 pages in length.

Writing in a journal changed my life. It was like housekeeping. If somebody told me a joke, I could write the joke down. My memory was cleansed, as I didn't have to burden my brain cells trying to retain odd bits of information. My productivity skyrocketed. And writing my thoughts down in a journal triggered other thoughts.

Some people say they don't have time to write in a journal. Hogwash. Everybody has time. You just have to take the time. Opportunities for writing abound. I will cite an example.

When my wife goes shopping, I can either walk the aisles with her or I can sit and write. I choose to write. She shops for 30 minutes, I write for 30 minutes. It's that simple. I find writing in a journal to be relaxing, rewarding, and productive. Ideas that had been ephemeral—elusive and fleeting images—are transposed into words. My mind becomes clear. Details are expressed and documented. My mental housekeeping allows me to take on new tasks. The old tasks are organized and set aside.

I started keeping journals in 1983. In the next 30 years I filled 22 volumes, some 6,600 pages. All journal entries are in ink. I always write in black ink, never blue. Blue ink does not photocopy well. If I ever get a ballpoint pen with blue ink, I throw it away.

The second thing that changed my life was my decision to get a quality pen—notably, a fountain pen. Ballpoint pens have become the norm. We take ballpoint pens for granted. That is a grievous mistake.

The pen of choice is a quality fountain pen. Fountain pens are a delight to write with. The ink as a fluid and lubricant allows the pen's tip to glide smoothly over the paper. Ballpoint pens drag and have to be pushed. I know that few will ever be convinced, but a whole new world awaits you. Go to a fine stationery store and try writing with a real fountain pen.

In the 1980s, I purchased a fountain pen for about $50. I guarded it carefully. I got years of enjoyment from my pen. Today it would be more costly, but still worth every penny.

A writing instrument is like a bed. You spend one-third of your life in bed. You deserve a decent bed. You also deserve a decent fountain pen.

Once you have your fountain pen, it is your pen. Never lend your pen to another person.

I regret that as my vision has diminished, I seldom write on paper. The keyboard and other electronic gadgets have invaded our world. Writing on paper becomes less and less frequent. That is indeed a shame.

Overestimating the Soviet Cold War Threat

FOR THE BULK OF MY YOUTH and adult years, our nation dealt with the Cold War—the Soviet and Communist expansion and threat. My mistake was my failure to not see the inherent flaws in the Soviet system and the factors that caused it to implode. In my lifetime, three people asserted that the Soviet Union and its threat would vanish.

In eighth grade, my social studies teacher was Mr. Ernest Schultz. He was a formidable man, a former World War II paratrooper. Mr. Schultz summed it up this way. The coalition of Russia and the Chinese represented the bulk of the communist threat. Schultz discounted the threat based on one simple fact— the Russians and the Chinese historically were rivals. No coalition of those two major powers would ever serve as a unified threat.

The second person who told me to not worry about the Soviet threat was Mr. Walter Kaufmann, a senior aeronautical engineer at Hughes Aircraft Company. Walt Kaufmann explained that a missile's ability to function—and thus attack America—depends upon literally millions of details working as planned. The Cold War would be decided based on economics. The side with the most efficient economic system would prevail. Walt Kaufmann concluded that we would win the Cold War, and without a shot or missile being fired. He made that observation in 1982.

I never met the third person who discounted the Soviet threat, but rather I read his remarks in his book. The man known as the Longshoreman Philosopher, Eric Hoffer, wrote his prediction in a diary entry in 1975: The Soviet Union would lose its grip on Eastern European countries and implode internally, and this implosion would take place in 1990. He was precisely on target. He published this in his book, *Between the Devil and the Dragon,* Harper Collins Publishing, 1982, a compilation of his diary and essay writings.

Even as the Soviet Union was imploding in 1989 and finally in 1990, I was in total disbelief. It was hard for me to realize what was happening. I had overestimated the Soviet threat. That overestimation was a serious error on my part. Peter O'Toole played the Roman Legion Commander in the 1981 television mini-series *Masada*. To paraphrase the Roman Commander at the movie's conclusion: It's a serious blunder to overestimate one's adversary. I made precisely that mistake in overestimating the Cold War era Soviet Union.

Right-Left Brain Test

IN THE 1980S, in my teaching and classroom conduct, I became emboldened to do as I pleased, with a focus on seeking truth. I explored a wide array of topics. It was common that I devoted five minutes at the start of each lecture to some sort of monologue where I would explore varied topics. I was challenging my students to think. Some students objected. These objecting students were what I classified as the memorizers. All they wanted to do was to memorize the factual materials to be able to regurgitate the memorized answers on the next test. Their only goal was getting an A. Truth and wisdom didn't appeal to them. Frankly, I wrote those types off and did what I wanted to do.

I suspected that just as people are either, for the greater part, left-handed or right-handed, the human body had other distinctions with R-L dominances. Humans, for example, like animals, are either right-eye or left-eye dominant. Rabbits can be easily tracked if you can ascertain whether the rabbit is left-eye or right-eye dominant. The rabbit will run away, but in a large circle. The rabbit hunter can just wait for the rabbit to appear again coming full circle.

Eye dominance is easy to test for in humans. Hold your hands outstretched. Bring your hands together to form a viewing hole about the size of a half-dollar. Look through the hole at some distant object. Then draw your hands closer to your face, while continuing to view the distant object. As your hands approach your face, the hole formed by your hands will converge onto one eye. That eye is your dominant eye.

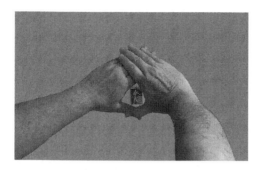

Now comes the topic of right-brained vs. left-brained dominance. I proceeded to search for a test. Right-brained people think sequentially. Left-brained people think pictorially, by manipulating and processing images.

My hypothesis is simple. I believe that because some people think differently, those people also learn differently. In my altruistic world view, if educators were on top of their game, the first act in teaching would be to determine each student's brain dominance. Most people are right-brain dominant. These people are auditory learners. Unfortunately, most isn't all. Some people are left-brain dominant. Left brain dominance suggests special thinking processes and learning by visualization. I believe I am left-brain dominant. I have concluded that my poor achievement in school was in large part due to being forced to absorb my lessons using language-based sequential or right-brain thinking. Oral instruction was Greek to me.

To be more precise, perhaps I should have said Latin. In ninth grade I struggled with Latin. In my sophomore year I took Latin II. The teacher was the archetypal battle-axe. Latin was obtuse for me. Since I was flunking, the school's guidance counselor, Ms. Ruth Cunningham, set up a meeting with my mother. Cunningham was another battle-axe, one who had been around so long she looked old in my father's high school yearbook, class of 1929.

I dropped Latin. That sealed my fate. College was no longer an option, as per what Ms. Cunningham proclaimed.

I wanted to be in shop classes, to run machines and build things. Instead, I was put into a government class. By my junior year, I was flunking English, a high school graduation requirement. I set my sights on joining the Army. High school graduation was in serious question. Unknown to me at the time, I was left-brain dominant. I see the world using images and relationships. In contrast, persons with right-brain dominance are auditory learners, as auditory is sequential in nature.

With this background in hand, I will return to my less than conventional classroom style. I was the professor in the classroom. What we needed was a brain-dominance test. The reality was clear to me. We as humans don't arrive with stickers on our foreheads declaring our brain-dominance type. Every person tends to live and think in their own bubble. It is a challenge to even understand that two brain dominance types exist, much less be able to self-diagnose.

I don't claim originality for the idea, but I can't find a source to quote. I had read of this test, but my contribution was in connecting the test to R-L brain dominance.

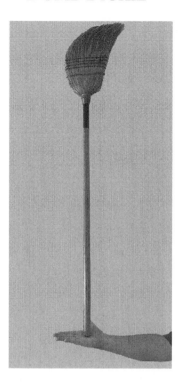

The Kleinian test involves balancing a broomstick. The broomstick is balanced under four different circumstances:

First, balance the broomstick using your right hand, obviously using your eyes for visual feedback information. The lower end of the broomstick can rest in your palm or on your fingertips. Be consistent as you perform the four balancing tasks.

Next, balance the broomstick with your right hand while reciting some verse or lyric by memory. The recitation can be "row, row, row your boat." It can be the Pledge of Allegiance. Mary Had a Little Lamb will work as well. Just try balancing while reciting something from memory.

Now, balance the broomstick using your left hand.

Lastly, balance the broomstick with your left hand while reciting something from memory.

The question boils down to which hand does better when the person is doing two simultaneous tasks—balancing and reciting from memory. My experimentation shows no distinction between right-handed and left-handed persons. The test works for all persons independent of right vs. left handedness.

I hypothesize the following: Left-brain dominant people will see a significant improvement in balancing with the left hand when also reciting from memory. Those who don't see the left-hand balancing improvement while reciting are right-brain dominant. My anecdotal tests show that about 15 percent of mechanical engineering students, about one in seven, are left-brain dominant. Please note that my tests were conducted with mechanical engineering students. That population may not be representative of the larger general population. I have no data to back up my next guess or stab, but I suspect that left-brain dominance in the general population is far less than the one in seven observed in my students. It stands to reason that people who think spatially will gravitate toward mechanical engineering, as they perceive that mechanical engineering is spatial in nature.

The reader is possibly wondering at this point how and why this test, if valid, works. The two halves or lobes of the human brain are connected, but by a limited bandwidth device or component. It is called the cortex.

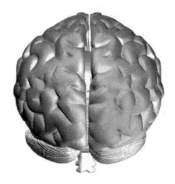

Messages have to pass back and forth between the two brain lobes. My hypothesis rests on the assumption that the act of reciting from memory has an amazing ability to relax or unclog the cortex, thus increasing its bandwidth. I have used the word bandwidth, as it is associated in communications with greater information transfer capacities. Somehow, people who are left-brain dominant see the benefit.

I am an empiricist. I frankly don't know all the intricacies of the human brain. Moreover, I don't care. My observations tell me one critical thing—that I am correct in my hypothesis. People who can improve left-hand balancing while reciting are left-brain dominant. I sought a test; I believe I found a test.

I also developed a second test based on color and pattern recognition. This book is published using only black and white illustrations to keep costs down. I will publish my second test when and if color illustrations become a cost-effective option.

My Failure to See the Future of Digital Computing

DURING MY TENURE as a professor at the University of Illinois, I was exposed to both digital computing and analog computing. Most people are familiar with the terminology of digital computing. Few understand the earlier form of computing, based on analogies and observing voltages in circuits to infer what an analogous outcome or response would be. In the 1970s, the University of Illinois was faced with demands by some engineering professors for better and more powerful analog computing devices. I was among those with interest in analog computers.

Analog computers were also referred to as electronic differential analyzers. Circuitry was designed to permit solutions of sets of differential equations. These devices mimicked the dynamics of physical devices under investigation. We used the phrase "hybrid analog computer." An administrative decision was made within the College of Engineering that only one hybrid analog computer would be purchased. It would serve all interested faculty across departmental lines. A committee was formed. I was the mechanical engineering representative on that committee.

I fervently believed that the future of computing, at least in my applications, would be done with such hybrid computers.

I never envisioned the growth and dominance of the digital computer. I never envisioned the Internet. And I never saw the coming of search engines such as Google.

I was immersed in science, engineering, and technology. It was a severe error on my part to be caught blind-sided by the advances in information technology. Even as I write in 2019, I am still amazed that I can key in just a few descriptive words and my Internet-connected computer will reply in seconds after having searched among perhaps a billion or so websites. I never saw it coming.

On the flip side, my life's work has produced fruit. My work in adapted bikes whereby kids with disabilities can master bike riding stands as one fruit. To date, the *iCan Bike* program has worked with roughly 30,000 children. That number increases yearly. Another fruit is my contributions to smart materials and intelligent structures. A third fruit stands as my analysis of Earth's climate dynamics. It was my background in analog computing that allowed me to make those advances. Not every problem encountered in life can be solved by digital computing. The areas of bicycle dynamics, tall building sway control, and the causation of Earth's glaciations are three such areas.

Albert Einstein remarked that a person is fortunate to have one original idea in their lifetime. I feel truly blessed as I can count my original ideas using my fingers on one hand. Now as I am in my retirement and golden years, I strive to document and publish the fruits of my analog computing-inspired contributions.

Now Comes the Bicycle

MY INTERACTIONS with the bicycle were deep and long. The time period from 1983 to 1990 saw an explosive growth in my research and my life's focus. I became obsessed in a quest to discover the hidden secrets of the everyday bicycle. The bicycle represented a paradox. It seemed so plain, visible, and obvious, but deep down its secrets were well hidden. About 20 research papers claimed to explain how and why a bicycle works. Alas, most of the papers were clearly wrong, as they stated conclusions that disagreed with the other papers. There was little consensus. In short, the scientific literature was in shambles.

My bicycle-related research was sparked in December 1982. Some of my students requested a better grade in my dynamic systems course. The course's subject matter was in understanding things that move and wiggle. Certainly, a bike moves and wiggles. It also falls down at times. I asked the students to write essays on how a bicycle stays upright. I liked the idea so much, the bicycle essay became a course requirement. That continued for about six years, which was twelve consecutive semesters. Because of large class sizes, about 600 or more students wrote these essays. It is difficult to condense six years of work into one section of this book; here is the condensed account.

The students typically worked in groups of three or four. In all, about 250 essays were turned in. Of those essays, half were doubtful, a quarter were sort of okay, and the final quarter of the essays were outstanding.

By the late 1980s, I had accumulated approximately 60 top-rank research papers related to the bicycle and its stability. I was sitting on more bicycle research than any other person in the world. To this day, I still retain copies of all those essays.

I have been asked why I didn't publish those findings or make them available to other researchers. In short, I would not and could not publish the work of my students without their permission. Also, a student essay might have stated claims, but I lacked absolute verification of those claims. In order to publish, I would have been obligated to replicate the experiments and findings, a daunting task. In 2005, I co-authored with two Swedish colleagues a paper subsequently published in the *IEEE Control Systems Magazine.* This paper reported on the best of the findings, the cream of the crop, so to speak. That paper received significant recognition and was later honored by IEEE as being the best paper out of several thousand published by IEEE that year.

In 1985, student complaints started to surface. I recall a discussion with one student in particular. He explained his dilemma. He intended to go on to medical school after engineering. He had to have an A in my course, but the essay assignment couldn't be completed by memorizing facts and repeating those facts back on an examination. Much of the existing literature on the topic was wrong, and so it was easy for me to spot students who merely repeated some published statement. They often became victims of my red pen.

I then proposed a solution. The student could saw a bicycle in half and make an experiment upon rebuilding the bicycle in some different configuration. Push the modified bike down a hill and report the outcome. Reality does not lie! Write the essay based on the outcome of an experiment. You can never be wrong.

I made a similar pronouncement openly in class. And so it happened that my students relied less on analysis and more on experiments. A phrase I coined was "Paralysis by analysis."

With these experiments, we were able to validate what initially started as theoretical insight. In the three main areas I researched in my life—control of tall buildings, glacial causation, and bicycle dynamics—the bicycle was possibly the most satisfying.

In contrast to the first two research areas (structural control and glacial causation), the bicycle represents a lone researcher's paradise. Bikes were plentiful. I could access bikes at will and for a modest budget. The time scale associated with a bicycle-related experiment was short. I didn't require the approval of an owner or city regulator. I didn't have to fight with politicians who have claimed the public policy related to climate change and global warming. The public didn't have life or death opinions about bicycles. Quite frankly, my dabbling into bicycle research was both harmless and even ignored and ridiculed by many. I had access to the necessary fabrication, notably machine shop tools, to make the experimental prototypes. Moreover, I induced my many students to take on the role of colleagues. Yes, some disgruntled students objected, but I had what I needed: sufficient numbers of capable and talented students who grabbed onto the idea of performing fun and yet groundbreaking research. Adding to all this, the bicycle literature was in chaos, as numerous papers had come to differing and even opposing conclusions.

Instead of adding to confusion, my students and I collectively started to come up with solid answers. This was what kicked my bike research into high gear. Given dozens upon dozens of experimental outcomes, the nebulous mystery of the bike came into clear view.

A seemingly obscure event took place in 1988. Although

obscure at the time, this near non-event played a significant role in future happenings. Students in my department at the University of Illinois would annually compete in American Society of Mechanical Engineering (ASME) speaking contests against teams from other schools. At that time I also served as the ASME student chapter's faculty advisor at the University of Illinois. That year we went to a regional ASME gathering in Louisville, Kentucky and took with us some research bikes to display and speak on.

A photographer from ASME took a picture of one bike that we claimed had zero-gyroscopic properties. It looked cool, and it got people's attention as well as sparking much conversation. The bike shown below is from one of my file photographs, but this wasn't the photograph published by ASME.

A photograph similar to my file photograph subsequently appeared in *ASME NEWS,* a society newsletter. A brief caption appeared with the ASME photograph. The caption stated that the bike had anti-gyroscopic properties and was a result of research at the University of Illinois. Beyond that, the photograph spoke for itself. The caption did not cite my name. That one photograph later, indeed years later, proved to be pivotal to the growth of the adapted bike program. Below, one of my students, Jadon Evans, is riding that bike.

The photograph shows the zero-gyroscopic bike. The correct word to use is "precession," but for many lay people the word precession doesn't make sense. Precession is a word from physics that denotes a reaction based on the conservation of angular momentum. The word "gyroscopic" brings to mind the image of a gyroscope. Because of this, I say things like zero-gyroscopic bike, but the correct terminology should instead be zero-precession. Hence, it is a zero-precession bike. The bike was not only rideable, it was, in fact, easily rideable. The two upper wheels rested on the two lower wheels and counter-rotated, which cancelled the precession effects.

What made this bike create such a stir was that many well-informed people bought into the common assertion often made by physics instructors: the spinning action of the wheel is what makes it possible to ride a bike. The important word in the assertion is the word "is." As various experiments attested, gyroscopic action (hence precession) is helpful in bike riding, but it isn't the one and only thing that causes a bike to be ridable. That *necessity* assertion was proved to be patently false. The physics instructors making such claims had previously jumped to a conclusion but never bothered to test the hypothesis with an actual bicycle experiment.

It is legend that introductory physics and science classes

demonstrate someone sitting on a stool while holding a spinning bicycle wheel. Spinning the wheel and being twisted about when the axle is inclined isn't the same as actually riding a bike.

What commonly occurs during the spinning wheel demonstration is that the physics instructor or some know-it-all adds the remark, "And this is why a bicycle works." My numerous experiments with real precession-canceling bikes smashed that assertion to bits and pieces. I found it amusing that once my students and I performed such experiments on real bikes all arguments were terminated.

One of my favorite expressions is, "Reality does not lie." Conduct an experiment and the outcome will always reveal the truth. In keeping with the spirit of empiricism, which is rooted in experimentation, my students created and tested an array of experimental bicycles under my supervision. Each experiment and its associated bike was constructed to solve and put to rest a specific bicycle-related mystery or issue. The results were outstanding to say the least. A number of experimental bikes focused on issues related to precession and the role of precession in bike riding.

As an example, the bicycle shown below was configured to find out if a person could ride a zero-precession bike (zero-gyroscopic) without hands. The student, Dave Nagreski, is shown riding the bike with ease while using hands. Our attempts to ride "no handed" were unsuccessful. In any event, I can assure my readers that whenever we took our bikes out for public demonstrations, the bikes were always crowd-pleasers.

The photograph below shows me along with many of the University of Illinois research bikes. This collection represented just some of the bikes built and submitted by my students. The date of the photograph is *circa* 1988-1989.

The above photograph was taken when I was about 50 years young. I didn't suspect it at the time, but as events unfolded, I found out I was suffering from Gull's disease. This is commonly known as hypothyroidism. I had gained weight. I was losing hair, noticeably on my eyebrows. I was becoming fatigued. I was experiencing short-term memory loss. Hypothyroidism is an insidious disease. It comes on slowly, taking years before making itself apparent. Few people recognize it, including doctors. Soon, in this Dumb Dickie saga, we will come face-to-face with my serious medical issues. Those medical issues brought the bicycle research activities to a stop. For now, let's keep pedaling our bikes.

One aspect of the bicycle research project focused on the matter of how children learn. Some students and I started to work with a handful of children around seven years of age. We would make an appointment with a parent and proceed to place the child on a bike and then launch the child. In the process of working with these children, my engineering students ended up doing a lot of running. We worked in the fall semester of 1986 with 10 children. Our observations were unexpected and even shocking. Nine of the children went through four distinct phases. Moreover, they each required approximately 44 minutes to master bike riding.

The tenth child also mastered bike riding but didn't progress through the four phases. In this case, the boy's father was present and shouting out commands and orders. My assumption at the time was that the child simply froze on the bike and did not attempt to steer or even pedal. Thus, the boy's arms remained locked at the elbows. After all, when children are subjected to a continual barrage of oral commands at a level they do not comprehend, they tend to freeze and do nothing. Much to our astonishment, as we approached the 44-minute mark, this last child went from doing nothing to virtual mastery of the bike in terms of steering, pedaling, and coming to a controlled stop.

We measured the time for each child by starting the clock when we first launched, then let the clock run continuously.

Thus, time spent walking back up the street's slight incline was also adding to the clock.

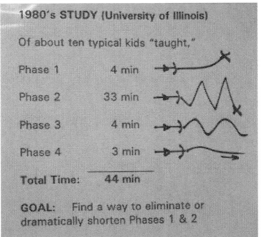

Of about ten typical kids "taught,"

1980's STUDY (University of Illinois)		
Of about ten typical kids "taught,"		
Phase 1	4 min	
Phase 2	33 min	
Phase 3	4 min	
Phase 4	3 min	
Total Time:	44 min	

GOAL: Find a way to eliminate or dramatically shorten Phases 1 & 2

The first two phases, which consumed 37 minutes, were typified by the bike oscillating and then falling over. It became obvious that one should modify the bike just as modern aircraft can be modified by what is called *compensation*. The goal became one of modifying the bike and hence the environment experienced by the child.

The objective became clear to me. The next step was to create a trainer bike with properly modified and more benign dynamics. Training wheels are deplorable. They make the bike rigid and precarious. What was needed was a way to allow the bike to act like a bike, but to slow down the action—to put the bike into a slow motion mode.

The trainer, if achieved, would function as a *stable attractor*, to borrow some terminology from chaos and fractal theory. Once stability could be assured, meaning that the bike wasn't continually falling over, the child's ability to adapt and learn would happen on its own and quickly. My task was reduced to a matter of making a trainer bike.

Hence, in 1987, I started my quest to design and build a trainer, a bike with modified (more gentle and benign) dynamics.

By this point in the spring of 1987, I finally understood why a bike behaves as it does.

I recognized that gravity was the central thing that dictated the quickness of the action, notably the fall. It was obvious that children had difficulty learning to ride because the timescale of action was too fast. I had to slow down the action, specifically the rate of fall.

One candidate solution would be to transport the children to another planet or our moon, a body that had a lower gravitational constant. I concluded that NASA wasn't interested. The second candidate solution was to have the kids ride bikes underwater so that the water would support the body's mass. I ruled that option out.

The third candidate option was to mitigate gravity itself. I had two obvious choices. The first was to use a wide tire similar in lateral profile to a rocking chair, allowing the bike to rock slightly side-to-side. Note that rocking chairs don't only rock, they simultaneously lift the occupant. This explains why rocking chairs typically don't fall over. The second way to mitigate gravity was to install compliant outriggers or spring-loaded training wheels. I chose to go down the path of using a wide tire, which was ultimately replaced in later designs by a hard, contoured roller.

Under my direction, several students constructed the first trainer. This bike used turf tires, those normally used on powered lawn mowers and garden tractors. Starting in 1987, I used the turf-tired trainer to work with children. The design used mechanical compensation techniques—I didn't feel that the world was ready for a high-tech electronically controlled and stabilized bike.

The results using the fat-tired bike were outstanding. Throughout the late 1980s and early 1990s, I worked one-on-one with perhaps 20 children. With each child, I gained experience. I became known as the Bicycle Doctor.

In the fall of 1992, I received a telephone call from California. The person calling was Grant Pedersen, now a legend in the world of bicycling. At that time, he was the head of Bridgestone Cycling in the USA, a branch of Bridgestone Tire Company based in Japan. Pedersen had been directed by his superior in Japan to contact me. The circumstances surrounding this telephone call were noteworthy and intricate. The man in Japan, it seemed, had seen the obscure photograph of the precession-cancelling bicycle published in *ASME NEWS* some four years earlier. The Japanese executive must have gone to some effort to identify me as the source and contact person. Recall that my name was not stated when the 1988 photograph was published by ASME.

The executive then directed Pedersen to contact me. Pedersen's first statement was, "I'm embarrassed. I've been told to call you, but I really don't want to talk to you." He probably hoped I would just hang up. If so, he could report back to his superior in Japan that he had tried and that I had refused to talk to him.

I didn't hang up.

After some time on the phone, I arranged to drive to a bicycle trade show to meet Pedersen in person. When I drove to Dekalb, Illinois, where the trade show was located, I took in my van some of the University of Illinois experimental bikes. Upon seeing the bikes, Pedersen became intrigued with the turf-tired bike and my stories about teaching children. It was agreed that I would write an article for the Bridgestone Cycling USA Magazine, of which Pedersen was the editor. Pedersen suggested that I submit an article of about 1,100 words along with a few black-and-white glossy photographs. Several weeks later, as agreed, I mailed the article and photographs to Pedersen. I heard nothing in reply for almost six months, so I literally forgot about having even written the article.

Recall that a complication of Gull's disease is often short-term memory loss. Strangely, I could still teach because my subject matter was related to long-term memory, for which I still had adequate retention.

Six months or so went by following the interchange with Pedersen. It was now getting into late February or March, 1993. A brown envelope arrived rather unexpectedly in the mail. Bridgestone Tire had suffered financial losses in Japan related to the devaluation of the Japanese yen, and Bridgestone had shut down its bicycle operations.

As a consequence, Pedersen was no longer employed by Bridgestone. But, because he loved bicycles, Pedersen opted to open his own bike shop in Walnut Creek, California. His newly opened shop published a small rag (a newsletter, or what is called a "house organ") called *The Rivendell Reader*. The article about my research with teaching children appeared, along with a photograph of my turf-tire trainer. In fact, my article appeared in one of the first issues of Pedersen's publication.

As the story behind the adapted bicycle research unfolds, we will again pick up the thread and significance of the Pedersen connection—an unlikely connection that followed events triggered by the seemingly obscure 1988 ASME article depicting the precession-cancelling bicycle. When the next connection comes some four years later, the chance circumstances are equally bizarre and improbable.

It became common that I was called upon to give presentations of the bicycle project and its findings. I also developed a bedside manner of using magic, or so I claimed, when working with children. Young children found me a large and foreboding figure. One way to alleviate that fear was to adopt a magician's role. Hence, I took to wearing a tall stove pipe hat.

One unexpected telephone call in April 1997 changed the course of my life. Two ladies in Toronto, Ontario, telephoned me. They were Barbara Anthony and Laura Hunter. They were therapists involved with kids with disabilities. The son of one of them had seen the *Rivendell Reader* story from the distant bike shop in Walnut Creek, published four years prior. Truth is stranger than fiction.

My head still swirls to think of the remote chain of events. An obscure ASME photograph from 1988, taken in Louisville, Kentucky, was noticed in Japan four years later. A Japanese executive directed Grant Pedersen to call me, which was the absolute last thing Pedersen wanted to do. I ended up traveling to Dekalb, Illinois, where I met him in person. Pedersen was subsequently discharged from his Japanese-based company, opened a bike shop in California, and published an obscure newsletter with a short article of mine. A young son of a lady in Toronto, half a continent away, in a different country and four years later, then told his mother. The mother called me on a whim.

I got the call a day or two after my forced and less-than-graceful retirement. My golden parachute, with its ink barely dry, gave me the time and funds to respond. On top of all that, my retirement agreement provided that all research bikes became my personal property. I thus had the key bike trainers to take with me to Toronto. It would be hard to make up these stories.

I was at a bike camp years later. While I was telling this story, a retired minister listened. He had brought his grandson to the adapted bike camp. The minister responded to me, "There are no accidents with God. This program is the ram in the bush." God provides for all His children. Children with disabilities have special needs. My program was the ram in the bush that God provided.

When the ladies called me in 1997, their one question was simple and direct, "Doctor Klein, can you teach children with disabilities to ride bikes?" With God, there are no accidents and coincidences. The call from these two therapists came on the heels of my ungraceful exit from the University of Illinois. God had closed one door, but simultaneously opened a second door. Not only was the second door opened, I was handed virtually everything required to tackle the next task.

At this point I feel compelled to make a dumb, but also possibly profound, observation. Contrary to most physical tasks that have to be learned and mastered, the human's ability to ride a bicycle comes as a sudden realization. The *Ah ha moment* triggers one key counterintuitive ingredient—to turn the bike's handlebars into the direction of the bicycle's fall. This realization happens in a brief moment and is totally opposite to the intuitive prior reaction of resisting the fall and thus turning away from the fall. The task of learning to ride a bike is in stark contrast to how humans learn most tasks involving motor plan development.

For example, jumping rope, swimming, catching a ball, throwing a ball, striking a pitched baseball with a bat, and countless other tasks are learned and honed far more gradually. Yes, exceptional people can do some of these things right away, and we describe these people as "naturals." Excluding the born naturals, most humans need considerable practice to master most skills involving human actions. In stark contrast for humans learning a task, learning to ride a bicycle represents something that happens over a vastly shorter time frame.

The question of whether a person can ride a bike or not has a binary answer. The answer is either yes or no. Once balancing is achieved based on steering commands, all other refinements like starting, braking, and navigation follow in rapid succession. It is only necessary for the learning rider to maintain speed and to nudge the steering into the direction of fall. Once basic balancing on a bike is achieved, the next step follows—and often within a few minutes.

I define the person attempting to teach a child to ride as the *spotter.* Unfortunately, numerous misinformed but otherwise well-meaning spotters do it wrong. These spotters don't understand what's going on. Far too many spotters insist on holding onto the bike. Yes, the bike and rider wobble in the initial moments following the launch. But the spotter's intervention is detrimental and counter-productive. The intervention causes a devastating diminishment in the rider's ability to refine their balancing skills. When spotting behind the learning child, it is obligatory that the spotter not keep grasping onto the bike, or training handle if so equipped. The erratic zig-zag pattern of the novice rider is quite natural and to be expected. The zig-zag stems from the time required for mental processing. If the spotter can just let go, the rider's zig-zagging will usually extinguish itself in minutes and without any intervention on the part of the spotter. After all, it is common knowledge that riding a bike is "as easy as riding a bike." Far too many people make far too much of something that is inherently so simple and natural.

I will return to the matter of bicycles later as this book's timeline unfolds. It is time to address my medical trials and tribulations.

Dr. Failure

As a pilot I was required by the Federal Aviation Administration (FAA) to pass an airman's medical examination every two years. Soon after moving to Champaign, Illinois, in 1968 I asked my flying friends who in our town among the FAA-certified physicians was the most strict and rigorous. I was given the name Dr. Harlan J. Failor. I proceeded to go to him for perhaps 20 years for my flight physical examinations. When I turned 50 in February of 1989, I was no longer flying actively, but I still continued to see Dr. Failor. It cost nothing extra, so I continued to request the airman's certification. That would allow me the option of taking up flying again if I ever desired. During this visit in February of 1989, I also asked Dr. Failor to do a general physical. He looked me over and ordered an array of the usual blood profile and urine tests. In about two weeks I received in the mail my new airman's medical certificate, signed by Dr. Failor. Dr. Failor was a quiet type with little to say. Knowing he was a man of economy of language, I automatically assumed I was in good health. After all, if one can qualify to fly airplanes then one is certainly in top condition. Unfortunately, that was not the case, unbeknownst to me at the time.

Almost two years later in December 1990, I was not feeling well. It was Sunday, December 23, just before Christmas. While rising to stand in church, I felt faint. Dr. Failor also attended our church, First Presbyterian Church in Champaign. I approached Dr. Failor during the coffee hour between services and told him I didn't feel well. His response was, somewhat coldly, "Please call my office and make an appointment to see me."

I knew at that moment I had to get past Failor to see somebody else. That afternoon Marjorie took me to the Carle Clinic Emergency Room in Urbana, Illinois. After explaining my symptoms to an intern, the intern replied, smiling, "Your diagnosis is actually quite simple." He opened up my chart and read a letter addressed to me and signed by Dr. Failor, dated 22 months earlier. Failor had signed the dictated letter in February of 1989 but then forgot to mail it to me. He had just closed my folder with the signed letter within. Any diagnosis by a physician is pointless if the diagnosis is not communicated to the patient for subsequent action. That failure constituted gross medical malpractice.

The essence of the letter was that I was suffering from hypothyroidism, known in medical terminology as Gull's disease. My case was advanced. The attending emergency room physician, Dr. Katheryn Wilson, had me admitted to Carle Hospital overnight. One reason for the hospital admission was to conduct more tests. She came several times to my bedside the next day as she did her rounds. On one visit, she came with a number of interns and residents. Her purpose was to show them a patient suffering from advanced hypothyroidism. She used the phrase "A constellation of symptoms."

I was discharged later that day, on Christmas Eve, so as to be home and with family for the holidays. Marjorie and I had planned a trip to Iowa. The doctors allowed me to go on that trip but cautioned that I needed to be guarded about being exposed to cold.

One of my symptoms was an enlarged heart. X-rays showed that my heart had expanded by 60 percent in volume. The intern joked, "You're a big-hearted guy." The heart expansion caused chest pains as my heart was trapped inside my rib cage. And the walls of my heart had become thin due to the expansion. I always reflect on the line near the end of the 1965 movie *Doctor Zhivago*, as Zhivago's half-brother explains after Zhivago's death on the streets of Moscow, "The walls of his heart were thin."

Hypothyroidism is an insidious disease. Its impact on the body is slow and gradual. Many people accept the symptoms as merely a part of aging, not suspecting a hormonal deficiency as the root cause. The tongue becomes enlarged. Skin and hair issues change one's appearance. There is shortness of breath and thus reduced physical agility. In my case, one devastating symptom was a loss in short-term memory. It is difficult as a professor to lecture effectively when one has impaired short-term memory. I also experienced weight gain, and at one point I reached 272 pounds. In comparison, my present weight is 202 pounds. My heart had enlarged as my body was fighting for oxygen. I became increasingly susceptible to cold, due to poorer blood circulation.

I ended up taking a partial medical leave for the spring semester of 1991 from the University of Illinois. I say partial, when in fact the department head graciously had me teach no classes. I got paid for showing up, so as to conduct research. The research was entirely at my discretion, so it was like having easy duty and no student load. My recovery took several years, if not more. Gull's disease is common and easily treated with a standard thyroid medication, but it must be treated. I will refrain from going into all the medical implications.

My advanced condition can now be traced to three systems that broke down, notably feedback systems. The irony was that I made my life's work based on expertise in feedback systems. The first system failure was that of my thyroid gland. The second failure was that Dr. Failor had diagnosed the problem, but had failed to intervene. His diagnosis was based on my extremely elevated TSH number (thyroid stimulating hormone). In February 1989, my TSH reading was 21.6, a number that is perhaps ten times beyond what would be considered normal. The TSH test is deemed to be incredibly reliable. There was no question about the diagnosis. The mistake on Dr. Failor's part was due, I assume, to his absentmindedness or preoccupation with other duties.

The third feedback system failure was my mistake as a patient. I failed to monitor my physician. I have now learned and apply this very simple rule in life—upon having medical tests done, if the doctor doesn't provide the test numbers, then take charge. One has to merely telephone the doctor's office. You then ask for the nurse, who will tell you the numbers. Actually, the numbers are irrelevant. What you really want to know is whether or not all numbers are within normal limits. My failure to monitor my physician cost me dearly. I lost multiple years of productivity.

I found out later that Dr. Failor's ineptness wasn't confined to me. He had developed a pattern of medical failures and malpractice, such that he was referred to by some as "Dr. Failure." Part of the problem was rooted in his advancement into an administrative role in Carle Foundation Hospital in Urbana. He had become preoccupied with counting pennies and saving money. I met with an attorney who handled medical malpractice cases. Three things made me drop that line of seeking redress: (1) Attorneys are even worse than doctors in terms of interactions, (2) it is exceedingly difficult to establish damages in a court of law over things so gradual, and (3) in spite of Dr. Failor's ineptness, the work done at Carle Foundation Hospital represents God's work.

Yet another observation: The medical profession is exceptionally protective of its own. For example, my file contained the original letter addressed to me in February 1989, but I was never allowed to see it, much less be given a copy.

Two Wrecked Cars

IN OCTOBER 1990, I had a relatively bad day. I was at home, preparing to drive to work. I received a telephone call from my daughter's school in Fisher, Illinois. My daughter Victoria, then age 17, had been in a rollover accident while driving to school. Her brother Timothy, then age 10, was also involved.

I drove to the accident scene. Vicki had become distracted. She lost control. The car, a Nissan compact sedan, had hit a shallow embankment, then tumbled like a football end over end. The car was sitting on its four tires some 365 feet from the roadway. There were no skid marks. The farm field had freshly been harvested of soybeans. One would expect to see gouges and skid marks in the soil. At first glance, it was a mystery. The car didn't fly 365 feet and just end up in a field.

"Your children were taken to Carle Hospital in ambulances," the deputy sheriff told me. That was in Urbana, Illinois.

"Do you have a cell phone I could use?" I asked. He did.

I called Marjorie at her school, in Champaign. I told her the simple facts: accident, both kids taken by ambulance, and both children alive to the best of my knowledge. The principal took over Marjorie's class and she drove to the hospital.

As Marjorie was looking for a place to park, the ambulances were unloading both of our children. Both were on stretchers.

Both children had been fitted with neck braces. I don't recall exactly, so let's add the usual IVs for extra drama.

Marjorie was so focused on her two children—while still driving—that she smashed into another vehicle and driver.

I had to deal with two children in the Emergency Room and two totaled car wrecks in the same day. At about noon, Tim asked for some food. That assured me Tim was okay. Victoria underwent various tests and some facial reconstructive surgery.

The sheriff's report stated that Vicki as driver was not wearing a seat belt, as she was found unconscious on the ground outside the vehicle. Police are probably nice people, but I have learned to be cautious and to examine the evidence myself. Vicki had a broken left collar-bone, typical of a seatbelt injury. She also had lacerations on her chin from impacting the steering wheel. The car keys had been removed from the ignition and were on the floor of the car. People thrown from a car don't take the time to turn the engine off and remove the keys. Vicki had done that out of reflex, then opened the car door, got out, and then lost consciousness.

Several months later I received a thin letter from my insurance company. The gist was that the insurance company no longer wished to carry my insurance.

I thank my guardian angel for being alert that day. The next spring, Vicki drove off a bridge, ending up upside-down and submerged at night in cold snowmelt water. Our guardian angel was again at work.

Cool Hand Luke and the IRS

THE BIBLE TELLS US to honor government and to render unto Caesar that which is Caesar's. That may be fine and well, but quite frankly, I don't like paying taxes. I have many strong objections to paying taxes and the Internal Revenue Service in particular. Some of my objections include:

- The IRS has computers and other practices in place to alert them if they suspect a taxpayer isn't paying enough. If the IRS was seeking fairness of tax payments, it would program its computers to check for both overpayments as well as underpayments. The IRS could easily adjust its search algorithms to check for fairness both ways—but they don't. Fairness in taxation is not their objective.
- The IRS tracks payment practices, looking for abrupt changes. If a taxpayer pays extra for years, but then tightens up, the IRS's algorithm will flag the taxpayer for a possible audit.
- The tax law requires that taxpayers testify against themselves. I consider that to be unconstitutional.
- In my case, I'm typically required to devote about a month of each year to record-keeping and other non-productive tasks. The IRS requires my servitude, but the IRS provides no remuneration for such services. I

consider this obligation to be involuntary servitude—something prohibited by the constitution.

- The government tells me that my taxes are used to help others who are less fortunate. If I help somebody out, in my altruistic mind I feel that I should get a thank-you letter. I have never received a thank-you letter from any beneficiary, nor a letter from the IRS itself.

- The IRS uses fear to increase the taxes collected. As an analogy, consider a tax-paying farmer with a fruit orchard. The IRS stands from afar, shouting and posturing. Many taxpayers comply out of fear or lack of any other choices. I choose instead to hang tough. The IRS will have to climb my tree and pick each piece of fruit.

In 1989 I was audited for tax year 1987. Below I have reprinted my journal entries documenting my experience.

1/27/89, Page 239

I received an audit notice from the IRS two days ago. They wish to audit 1987. Actually, I am in pretty good shape for 1987 except that I'm not experienced in the fight. It seems that the IRS computer flagged the audit due to a discrepancy in home maintenance interest. I believed that Champaign National Bank neglected to send a 1099-INT, and thus the IRS computer flagged the $5,000+ "error." It seems that they will now audit the return in a wide range of aspects.

5/16/89, Page 280

I finished my IRS audit yesterday. Ron Kiddoo (CPA) eased my concerns and went with me. The auditor, Barb Schweitzer, was polite, young, and a better-than-average bureaucrat. She was a check and pick auditor: She wanted to see receipts/cancelled checks. I was able to field every request for specific documentation.

She was concerned with respect to:

1. Some of my classifications
2. Profit motive

About halfway through I sensed that she was wrapping up for exit. There was "no change," thus the audit was a major victory for my side. The spreadsheets were very valuable, along with the ability to provide corresponding check numbers and, at times, receipts. All the way home I sang the line from Cool Hand Luke, "Yeah boss! I got my mind straight. I won't back sass no more. I got my mind straight boss! Don't hit me no more boss!"

As I had approached the audit, I reflected on how ironic it was that I entitled my autobiography "Mathematics, Philosophy, and Form 1040." As I've given talks to hundreds of people on tax strategies, certainly I had to win this particular battle.

Kiddoo served to see that nothing got out of control—sort of like backup in loading cattle. The trick is to contain things so that there is no outbreak or fire. We don't want to be adding visible damage control. I recall that Kiddoo aided on several points:

1. Reflection in 1985's $87,000 loss in that other schedules showed profits.
2. That the utilities were due to telephone, not power. Kiddoo didn't want to fall into the "office in the home" trap.
3. When a big item was not depreciated, Kiddoo pointed out that the Section 179 expense was not filled. The audit was a broadening experience.
4. That the "writing" expenses were minimal with respect to the whole and thus not worth picking apart.

About the IRS audit, she asked for verification on big items like:

- Monitor – alias Sony 19" TV set

- Spritz – a serving tray
- Test equipment – scales (antiques)

She never questioned why I needed scales or a monitor, or why a monitor cost $750!

As I reflect back on my audit and the IRS in general, I recognize that they are a low-budget operation. Those who conduct audits are generally young and lacking in experience. This stands to reason. An IRS employee who becomes proficient will gravitate to private practice. The now former IRS employee can make far more fighting the IRS by representing taxpayers.

As a taxpayer, I had a tremendous edge over the auditor. I had spent my life focused on my affairs. In contrast, the IRS auditor had to come up to speed with little knowledge of how I conducted my affairs.

Another point is that the best way to minimize taxes paid is to have less income. This might sound like an oxymoron, but it isn't. The trick is in conducting one's affairs using a small business or LLC. Yeah Boss. I got my mind straight. I won't back sass no more.

The Deluxe Deer Blind

As my health issues stabilized in the mid-1990s, I took a greater interest in deer hunting. Marjorie and I were still living on our hobby farm, 40 acres in Champaign County, Illinois. The 40 acres met the legal requirement to be classified as a farm, at least concerning deer tags. As a resident landowner, each person living on the property was entitled to two free deer tags, I merely had to apply for them. And as residents we did not have to buy hunting licenses and habitat stamps, as long as we hunted on our property. My daughter, Vicki, was by then married and away, but we had three residents: Marjorie, Tim, and me. We had a green light to shoot as many as six deer per season.

I decided to build an elevated deer stand. It was located at the far northwest corner of our property. Deer traffic was heavy, as the neighbor's woods funneled deer past my deer blind. This deer blind was actually my third iteration. Hence, in the family we dubbed it the "deluxe deer blind."

Cost of materials and my time were not constraints. I located four used utility poles and put each into a hole dug with a tractor-mounted PTO posthole digger. I then bolted some sturdy cross supports, typically 2"x10" lumber. Diagonal cross-bracing prevented side-to-side sway. The height above ground level was dictated by the reach of the hydraulic loader on my

John Deere 70 tractor.

I constructed the deer blind itself in my barn, where I had electrical power, tools, and lights. The deer blind was 4' by 4' in footprint. The sides were ¾-inch sheet treated plywood. The roof was in the usual peaked gable shape. I used tab shingles to make it watertight. Each of the four sides had two window provisions. A framed window could be opened and held in the open position. Each window also had sliding plexiglass clear panels and a sill where I could place a sandbag. The use of a sandbag helps immensely in steadying a gun.

The hunter would sit on a swivel office chair. I had some shelving overhead for supplies, snacks, and such.

When the deer blind was finished, I hoisted it up inside my barn's center aisle and lowered it onto a flatbed trailer. Then I drove out to the corner of my lot to hoist it into position.

I used the hydraulic loader on the John Deere 70. I caught the close end with the leading edge of the loader. I then used a come-a-long to keep the overhanging deer blind from falling as I lifted it with the loader.

Within a short time, the deluxe deer blind was in place. Using sturdy #9 wire, I wired it securely to the support beams, lest some heavy wind think about blowing it off. I secured some heavy plywood as a front entry, then wired an aluminum ladder in place to allow the hunter to ascend and descend at will. I stocked it with supplies, including the swivel chair and a few sandbags.

A common cause of hunter injury is falling out of trees. I designed the deluxe deer blind to be safe. I used a sturdy ladder, wired securely in place. Once up the ladder, the hunter could stand on a secure and level platform. From there the hunter could open the door to the blind and step in. I designed the deer blind to be comfortable while seated. Staying warm was never a problem. The hunter in full hunting gear sat wrapped in a sleeping bag. I never got cold when snug in a sleeping bag in the deluxe deer blind.

The floor of the deluxe blind was up about 14 feet. The hunter's eyes were about 18 feet above ground. All shots at deer were downward, with the ground as the ultimate safety device. Bullets didn't fly into the air and hit innocents. When a deer was hit, the elevated position allowed the hunter to observe the movements and direction. Getting lost in the woods wasn't an issue. I had a clear view of my house.

Hunting in the deluxe deer blind was enjoyable and successful. I shot perhaps 20 deer. My son, Tim, and his friends shot that many or more. After a deer went down, we always took the easy route. I usually walked to the barn and returned riding the JD-70 with its loader. After tagging and field-dressing the deer, I would hang the deer in the center aisle of the barn.

Our practice was to shoot all legal deer. We took no live

prisoners. Fawns and does made good freezer treats. Of the meat we consumed, well over half was venison.

The Illinois Department of Conservation encouraged farmers to thin out the deer population. In Illinois at that time, five animal species were out of control: white-tailed deer, Canada geese, raccoons, possum, and beaver.

In the U.S., deer are responsible for as many as 350 human deaths annually. A typical deer-car accident costs about $5,000. I did my public service. In my hunting career, I have harvested 26 deer. I define a harvested deer as one I was able to hang in the barn on a hook.

Tim became an excellent marksman. He took the hunter safety course. He bagged his first deer at age 13. It was a young thing. He told me it was a doe. When I field-dressed it, I came upon a pair of testicles. I explained to Tim that he had shot a button buck. He replied, "That makes me feel better." Tim obviously wanted to tell his schoolmates he had shot a buck.

A year later in the fall of 1994, Tim shot a deer through the heart at 156 yards. Thereafter, whenever I tried to counsel him on some finer points of hunting deer, he wasn't interested in advice from his father. Tim said, "Dad, I can shoot them through the heart at 156 yards." I was without a reply. Tim's record distance with shotgun slug stands at 213 yards. That represents an amazing feat as most people consider the shotgun's effective range to be about 100 or 125 yards. We do use sabots in rifled barrels. I have observed that technology advances far faster than legislation. Modern shotguns and sabots can outperform what used to be the standard deer cartridge, the .30-30.

Tim became an incredible shot and successful deer hunter. He would shoot them faster than I could field dress and process them.

As a side note, I had placed yard-marker signs in the open fields in three directions. I didn't have to guess the range of a deer when it stood next to a sign saying "75 yards." It is my understanding that deer don't read well.

I waited in a prime location for deer to come past me.

Deer hunting requires both desire and skill. The essence of skill is the discipline to not make mistakes. When you make the slightest mistake, the deer pick up on it and depart. They are called white-tails. You see a white tail bounding away and well beyond gun range.

Deer have incredible ways to detect danger. Hearing and smell are intensely acute. In contrast, deer have limited vision. Yes, they can see, but their sight serves them to warn of only certain things:

- Movement
- The face of predators—be it dogs, wolves, or humans with a pair of eyes and a nose looking at them
- The human profile

Deer can't see a human if the human is blended in with a large tree trunk or boulder. I've had deer walk past me at a distance of ten feet. I remained motionless. I was in plain sight. Before you turn your head to scan about you, you use only eyeball movement, then slowly turn your head. That one deer never sensed my presence. In that case the wind was blowing towards me. Deer are color-blind.

Excuses as to why the deer got away don't count. You either get the deer, or you don't.

I learned how to butcher from my father-in-law. On the farm in Iowa we butchered a cow each winter. Deer are nothing more than little cows. All the butchering steps follow the same principles. My father-in-law and brother-in law Edwin are shown in the photo below doing the skinning. I was behind the camera.

Of all my attempts at seeking hunting companions, virtually all failed. I can name a few exceptions, like Tom Jensen, Gus Hatch, and my son, Tim. Gus Hatch, a friend of Tim's, was the finest tracker I've ever met. I always joked that Gus was an Indian trapped in a white man's body.

Many of the others were jerks. They preferred to smoke and talk loudly while expecting to not be heard, couldn't read a compass if their life depended on it, and couldn't hit anything with a rifle or shotgun. Some thought the best part of deer hunting was playing cards at night, smoking, drinking, and leaving a stack of dirty dishes in the sink. When it came time to drive deer, they couldn't slam a truck's door louder if they tried.

Building the deluxe deer blind in my own private hunting preserve solved a long-standing problem: I no longer needed hunting companions. I became a lone hunter.

I'll end with this: There are two types of people in the world—deer hunters and everyone else.

Golden Parachute

I DIDN'T PLAN my retirement. Others caused it to happen, and quite suddenly. When I joined the University of Illinois as an Assistant Professor in 1968, the Department Head, Dr. Helmet Horst, made one point: Do not pursue outside funding. Korst recognized that my greatest contribution would be my thoughts. If I had outside research contracts, I'd end up writing reports nobody would ever read. Korst highly valued my ability to think and to publish scholarly papers. I also handled the teaching load in control systems. Most other mainstream ME courses required four or five devoted faculty. I am proud of the fact that the ME department at Illinois surged in national rankings, from ninth prior to my arrival up to third. Upon my retirement in 1998, the ME department at Illinois had eclipsed the ME department at our icon rival, M.I.T. In stating rankings, I have relied on U.S. News and World Report findings. The only two schools ahead of the ME department at Illinois were Stanford University and UC-Berkeley. In order to achieve such a high ranking, a department had to be strong in all areas. For my three decades at Illinois, I was instrumental in lifting the area of control systems to a position of national and world prominence.

Department Heads come and go. As the years went by, the rules for success changed. The pursuit of outside funding became king. As the twig is bent, so grows the tree. I didn't change. I didn't want to. My roots and habits were set.

The students also changed. As Illinois gained in national ranking, the students came expecting A grades from a top school in order to get a prestigious position upon graduation. The pursuit of truth and wisdom didn't interest them. But I didn't play the memorization game. A crisis erupted on March 21, 1997.

A group of disgruntled students sought a meeting with the Department Head, Dr. A. L. "Tad" Addy. Later that day, I was summoned to Dr. Addy's office. It was a bare-knuckles showdown meeting, hardball and ugly. As I was a tenured professor, firing me was beyond Addy's reach, but he was prepared to make life uncomfortable for me.

I solved his problem and mine. I agreed to resign. Addy had a golden parachute for me in exchange. If I agreed to retire, my take-home retirement benefit represented a 20 percent pay increase. By retiring, I was getting a substantial raise and I never had to go to work again. I asked only one question: "Where do I sign?"

The disgruntled students must have been overjoyed to both do me harm and to see me gone. I doubt if they ever realized what an incredible favor they had done for me.

As I walked out the building, I smiled and never looked back. I had three things: time, adequate cash flow, and a base on which to build grander things. For two years, from 1998 to 2000, I served as chair for a local gun-rights advocacy group. Membership expanded five-fold under my helm. It has since reached regional and even national standing as Guns Save Life, Inc.

I was also able to develop the national adapted bicycle instruction program, now administered by a parent-based charity, iCan Shine, Inc. To date, that program has served roughly 30,000 children with varying disabilities.

As an annuitant with the State of Illinois, my annuity is locked into compounded three percent per annum increases. At the University of Illinois, the budgets were too tight for such annual increases. In the years following my exit, the tighter budgets would have never afforded me my golden parachute. My retirement was a once-in-a-lifetime opportunity. Marjorie and I are not rich, but we are as well-off as we ever dreamed. Life is good. I am having a ball. As I wake each day, my mind is awash with far more ideas and adventures than I could ever manage to handle.

The Adapted Bike Program

FOLLOWING MY UNGRACEFUL but lucrative exit from the University of Illinois, I embarked on my next goal: the development of a national adapted bicycling instruction program for children with disabilities. I spent time in 1997 and 1998 in Toronto, Ontario. This opened my eyes to the need for a program devoted to teaching children with disabilities. However, my border crossings were far from pleasant experiences. In August 1998, when I finally managed to exit Canada, I enjoyed my drive west through Michigan on my way back to Illinois and home.

For the next 20 years, I devoted my energies to the development of the program. I designed and produced my own line of adapted bikes. The central workhorse was the roller bike. A second unique bike was the dual tandem trainer. I produced a dual tandem trainer of a new design in 2012.

Each fleet of adapted bikes is comprised of 27 bikes, each bike having a unique purpose. In all, I've built 15 working fleets. Each fleet is hauled in a dedicated enclosed cargo trailer.

At present, the program is only offered in North America. Inquiries have come in from overseas, notably places like Sweden, the United Kingdom, and Australia. A day will hopefully come when children all over the world can be served, but that day isn't at hand, at least not for now. I feel blessed to have been an instrument in bringing this program to fruition.

As of this writing, the adapted bike program serves approximately 3,000 children annually. Camps are scheduled across the United States and into Canada.

LOOKING BACK ON A LIFETIME

Philosophical Musings Across Eight Decades, and Counting

Uncovering Kristallnacht's Secret

THIS DUMB DICKIE STORY centers around an engraved Nazi presentation pistol.

In the past hundred years, some dates and events stand out. I will name three: Kristallnacht on the night of November 9, 1938; the Japanese attack on Pearl Harbor on December 7, 1941; and more recently the terrorist attacks on September 11, 2001.

The events throughout Germany and Nazi-occupied Austria on the night of November 9, 1938 were dubbed as "the night of broken glass," or in German, Kristallnacht. My name is Dumb Dickie. I was still being carried in my mother's womb on that fateful date. Notwithstanding, I ended up playing a critical role in the Kristallnacht events. I will now tell my story.

On that night, throughout Germany and Austria, Nazi brown shirts smashed as many as 30,000 Jewish-owned shops, businesses, and synagogues. Soon thereafter, Germany's Supreme Court Justice ruled that Kristallnacht was caused by the Jews. Fault was placed on the Jews, with their citizenship being the end target. The judge who rendered that ruling was Walter Buch. Buch's ruling became the basis for the Third Reich's confiscation of Jewish properties. Jews were rounded up and relocated into ghettos, usually within major cities. All of this happened to legitimize the seizure of Jewish properties, to cause many Jews to become forced laborers, and to send Jews to the now infamous Final Solution. Six million Jews were estimated to have died in the Holocaust. Again, Kristallnacht was the start, the genesis of the Holocaust. I want to tell you a story underpinning Kristallnacht. I want to explain the genesis of Kristallnacht.

Walter Buch

The story focuses on an engraved Nazi Walther Model PP pistol. Nazi big-shots enjoyed ceremony and especially ornate engraved weapons of war. Engraved swords, daggers, and sometimes pistols were treasured and symbolic gifts. Gifts of this magnitude from Nazi to Nazi were not given so much for thanks and recognition of past faithful service, but rather as bribes for some future service. The donor commonly expected something in return, a favor to be called for later. I happen to be the present owner of one specific Nazi gift.

I have no paperwork or documentation. Allied bombers, especially the British, destroyed factory after factory. All production records for Walther firearms were destroyed. Some documentation exists on the pistol itself. The pistol was engraved with the date November 5/6, 1938, the donor's signature, and the recipient's initials, "WB."

My father, Albert Klein (1910-1993), brought that pistol home in the autumn of 1953. He paid $75 and had it wrapped in a standard shop rag. Pop laid the pistol on the table in front of us, as if he had a winning Pinochle hand. He had returned after being on a job in the Akron, Ohio, area. Pop traveled frequently for Bullard Machine Tool Company. Obviously, Pop purchased the Walther pistol from the American officer, now a factory worker or boss, who had accepted the surrender of the recipient "WB." I assert that the German big-shot was none other than Nazi Germany's Supreme Court Justice, Walter Buch (1883-1948). Based on the engraved signature, the donor was Fritz Sauckel, the Nazi Minister of Labor. Perhaps it would be more correct to say forced labor.

Fritz Sauckel

Fritz Sauckel was not a nice man. He was in charge of supplying Nazi Germany with volunteer laborers, most commonly from Eastern European countries that the Nazi Blitzkrieg had overrun and occupied. It is fair to say that as many as 300,000 forced laborers died under the most horrible of conditions. When a worker died of exposure, malnutrition, or exhaustion, he or she was replaced with yet another volunteer.

Fritz Sauckel was tried at Nuremberg. He and ten other Nazis were sentenced to death. Hermann Goering escaped the hangman by swallowing a smuggled cyanide tablet. Fritz Sauckel was the second Nazi hanged in the wee hours of October 16, 1946. The hangman, Master Sergeant Robert Woods from San Antonio, Texas, had a special treat in store for Sauckel. The hangman's rope was short. Some considered it an inadvertent mistake. I don't. Woods was an experienced hangman, having practiced on several hundred before Sauckel's turn. The drop did not break Sauckel's neck. He was strangled as he dangled and squirmed. Because time was short and other Nazis had to be hanged, Woods and his assistant finally grabbed Sauckel's legs, pulling him downward.

Walter Buch was tried and sentenced by a post-Nuremberg German court to prison. In November 1948, Buch committed suicide by slitting his wrists and jumping into a lake.

Over the years that my parents had the pistol, it was not considered valuable or unusual. It was merely prettier than most other firearms. My mother kept it loaded in her bedroom, for possible self-defense. Mother, being Danish, abhorred all things reminding her of the Nazi occupation. I got the engraved Walther pistol from her after she asked me to see that all remaining firearms were no longer accessible to my father. Pop's dementia and his hostility to others concerned her. Even by the early 1960s, sadly Pop's mental state and vision were in decline.

It wasn't until about 1999, following my retirement, that I showed the pistol to a friend. The friend, Frank Wright, knew more about Nazi history than me and identified the signature of Fritz Sauckel.

Several firearms collectors and historians have authenticated both the pistol and Sauckel's engraved signature. Both experts offered to purchase the pistol, then in five figures. I declined. Internet research at that point became cake.

The presentation date coincided with a large Nazi Gautag (party day) in Weimar, Germany. Weimar was Sauckel's base of operations. Hitler was present. Churchill had just recently denounced Hitler in a speech in the British House of Commons. In Hitler's broadcast rebuttal speech at Weimar, he denounced Churchill as a war-monger. Churchill was on target. Hitler's armies invaded Poland less than a year later, on September 1, 1939. The invasion of Poland officially started World War II. Churchill later wrote that he wanted the war to be named "the unnecessary war." He had urged Britain to nip Hitler in the bud in the mid-1930s, thus preventing the war from happening. If the Treaty of Versailles had been enforced in 1936, WWII would have been avoided.

My research has shown that approximately 10 Nazi big-shots had the initials WB.

Most of the 10 were military officers. My research established that the pistol was engraved for a civilian recipient, as ranking

Nazi generals typically were given pistols engraved with their names in full, not abbreviated. Other factors also pointed to Buch, making him the obvious recipient.

My research suggested that Sauckel gave the gift to Walter Buch as a bribe. The bribe was for a favorable Supreme Court ruling that would give Sauckel access to what he desperately needed: confiscated Jewish factories and more forced laborers.

Now, ask yourself these basic questions:

- How often can a person own or even handle a pistol that can be associated with an incredibly notorious criminal?
- How often can one own or even handle a firearm documented to have been in the possession of and given as a gift by a criminal hanged at Nuremberg?

Sauckel's engraved signature stands as absolute and unquestionable validation of the firearm's authenticity. In the case of Fritz Sauckel alone, he was responsible for the deaths of hundreds of thousands of people. As a fugitive following the war, he was caught hiding in a cave in Bavaria. He was tried at Nuremberg and hanged. After his hanging, his body was cremated. His ashes were strewn in a ditch somewhere in Germany on a rainy and cold night. The location was kept secret lest some future Nazis attempt to build a monument in his honor.

My assertion that Buch was the recipient is based on circumstantial evidence, not solid evidence. The Nazis were big on ceremony and taking photographs. Close to 100,000 Nazi photographs survived the war. As historians uncover and document the photographs, I anticipate the day when somebody with better eyesight can find the photograph showing Sauckel handing the presentation pistol to Buch, with Hitler standing among them smiling. I consider November 1938 to be the high tide mark of the Third Reich. The Kristallnacht bribe pistol sealed the fate of millions upon millions.

I made many mistakes over the 65 years that the Klein family has had possession. I myself have had the pistol for over 40 years. I was so dumb that I used to carry the pistol for self-defense. I even fired it and failed to properly clean it afterwards. I assumed that anybody with the first name of "Fritz" had to be a nobody. For decades, I left the pistol in some obscure drawer.

One would have to search far and wide to come up with a firearm or artifact that can come close to matching the significance of this one. Perhaps Oswald's Italian rifle might be a candidate. But that rifle killed just one man, not hundreds of thousands and even millions.

Well, I'm going to take a nap at this point. I've never had a bad nap in my entire lifetime.

My Affinity for Country Western Music

As a kid, I was early on attracted to the romance of the old west, notably through music. A favorite song of mine, popular in the post-war era, was *Ghost Riders in the Sky*. The prominent vocalist at the time was Vaughn Monroe (1911-1973). Another popular song of that era, again a favorite of mine, was *Cool Water*. I will mention yet another, *Tumbling Tumbleweeds*.

One reason I still like country western music is that it can take one's mind off the ever-depressing daily events. I find the present cultural divide in our nation gloomy at best. Country western music takes me away from all that. Songs can focus on absurd things like my dog has fleas, and watching your hat on the hat-rack.

I like country western songs for another reason: their philosophy of life. A favorite sung by Kenny Rogers is *The Gambler*. Every hand's a winner, every hand's a loser. Know when to hold 'em; know when to fold 'em; know when to walk away. I fervently believe the song's lyrics to be true.

My life has had incredible ups and downs. Despite hard times, the ingredients are there for each person to make something of themselves. Recently, I met a young man, age 19. The boy, and yes I'll call him a boy, said, "I never learned to ride a bike. My father never taught me." To me, anybody who is 19 and physically fit has total control of their future. Borrow somebody's bike and just start pedaling!

Music soothes and relaxes me. To my ears, the world's finest vocalist is Roberta Flack. Two of her songs are *Killing Me Softly* and *The First Time Ever I Saw Your Face*. Her songs and voice are exquisite. I also enjoy the songs of John Lennon.

When I have the radio on in the shop, two things will make me turn to another station or turn the radio off. One is rap music. The second is the sound of someone laughing as a commentator is speaking. I can't even hear what's so funny over all that laughing. I am in control of the dial and power switch.

The issue of athletes taking a knee isn't a part of my life. I watch zero professional sports. Somebody would have to pay me to go to any professional sporting event, and I mean big dollars. I value my time. Time is precious to me.

Einstein once made an appointment to have dinner in London with a man. The two agreed to meet at a bridge. The other man was detained. Hours later, he went to the bridge. Einstein was still there. The man apologized profusely.

Einstein replied, "I can do my work anywhere." Einstein enjoyed being left alone; alone to think. Einstein's task in life was to be able to think.

I also feel that thinking is my primary function in life. I feel incredibly blessed to have had an occupation that paid me just to think. I also felt blessed to be immersed in a sea of so many sharp young minds. As for my engineering colleagues, there were some real diamonds. Jim Leach, Douglas Marriott, and Branny von Turkovich stand out. As for the rest, I wouldn't give a nickel for the bulk of them. Mechanical engineering professors are pretty lackluster. I'm also sure they dislike country western music.

Revealing My Brain Wiring

I CONTINUE to do dumb things. One recent dumb thing was that I wrote this book, *Dumb Dickie.* I will explain.

It is a mistake when one pens an autobiography. It might be okay, but an author should release it only posthumously. When one is still living, the autobiography provides your enemies and adversaries with sordid details as to how you, as author, think and react in crisis situations. Enemies can effectively attack you because they can predict in advance how you, as the targeted victim, will react in any given situation.

I am reminded of the line in the movie *Patton,* where Patton is first engaging Rommel in the African desert: "Rommel, you magnificent bastard! I read your book."

Yet Another Early Mistake

As I reflect on my life, it is easy to be considered a failure. Failing is easy, anybody can do it. You don't have to try. You don't find books in libraries on how to fail. Succeeding is hard, or at least harder. It is easy to fail, it is easy to give up. It is easy to underestimate yourself.

One consistent trait I exhibited in my life was to underestimate myself and my ability.

You can't pick your parents and family, but you can pick your friends and mentors. I once heard the expression, "If you want to be a big flea, hang around big dogs."

Subroutines as a Way to Combat Dumbness

AS I REFLECT BACK, a mistake in my life was being oblivious to the concept of modular thinking. I finally became firmly aware of the concept in graduate school. The introduction to subroutines as used in FORTRAN programming made clear to me what I call modular thinking and its incredible benefits. I was exposed to subroutines initially in the spring of 1964, when I took my first graduate classes at Penn State. The word "subroutine" became hardwired into my thinking processes, so I prefer to continue its usage. I recognize that the younger generation now prefers words like *routine* and *function* as the meaningful equivalent.

As an illustration from my pre-subroutine days, I decided early on to take the engine out of my car. This was my very first engine removal attempt. I was 16 or 17 at the time. After opening the hood, I proceeded to just start removing parts. If I saw a part that could be removed, such as the air cleaner, I removed it and set it aside. Perhaps the spark plugs came next. At some point I drained the radiator and saved the coolant in a drain pan. I arranged all the removed parts in a row on the garage floor so that I could reinstall them later in the proper order. What later dawned on me was the concept of removing an engine as a modular or intact unit of parts.

Modular thinking has become central in my approach to dealing with life's problems and varied challenges. Without doubt, I could fill volumes just talking about how I use prepared, stored subroutines to solve a myriad of daily problems. When I receive a thin and unfriendly letter from the IRS, I have a prepared subroutine or response. When I get pulled over in a traffic stop, I have a precise subroutine for my conduct and answers. When I try to order from a menu in a dark restaurant, I have a prepared subroutine. When somebody is driving behind me too close to my bumper, I have a subroutine. When I interview for a job or visit some commercial establishment as a guest, I have a subroutine. When I am gassing up and get solicited by a panhandler, I have a subroutine. I have a subroutine for how to bid at auctions. If I ever feel threatened when in some unfamiliar spot, I have a prepared subroutine.

For the sake of having a little fun, I'll go into the situation of being served at a restaurant. Bear in mind, just as I have prepared subroutines, so have others. Moreover, others are commonly using their subroutines against me. After a waiter or waitress serves you your food, he or she will usually come back to check on you. If done properly, this will happen after you have taken your first bite. The waiter asks, "Is everything okay?"

Most people, being trained to be civil and polite, answer, "Oh yes, everything is fine." My instincts see this as a trap. When you dine out you are entering into a legal agreement. You will be given a bill. You, in turn, expect wholesome food served in a safe environment. When and if you reply in the affirmative, you are admitting that you have inspected the food and have deemed the food to be safe and satisfactory. But you haven't finished your meal. In the next bite you could come upon a piece of broken glass. That is unlikely, but it does allow me to make my point.

The mistake in being polite and answering in the affirmative is simple. You have ceded rights and have gotten nothing in return. As per my prepared restaurant subroutine, I resort to a different strategy. My most common reply is, "It's too dark in here. I can't see."

Should the waiter continue to ask about the food, I then resort to, "It smells a little funny. Do you think it's all right?"

When I deal with a hardcore waiter hell bent on an answer, I go to my third level. At this point I usually have my journal out. I am writing a few notes.

"Sir, just checking in again to see that everything is okay?"

"I can't tell you right now," I'll reply, still writing.

"Oh, um, is there a reason you can't tell me? I really just want to be sure everything is okay."

"You can read about it later," I'll say, maintaining a straight face.

My subroutine ploy causes the waiter to eventually assume I am a foods column reporter for a regional or area newspaper. I haven't used this ploy often, but when I do, excitement and panic happen. The waiter in one case informed the restaurant manager. The manager came to the table and personally apologized for the delay, as my meal that day took a long time to arrive. When it came time for the bill, I was told that the manager wanted everyone at my table to be his guests that day. Bear in mind that a poor newspaper report on a restaurant will have devastating repercussions on that establishment.

One of my favorite subroutines is what I call the People Matrix. For simplicity, look at two attributes or qualities in people. One attribute is competence. The lack of competence is incompetence. The second attribute is aggressiveness or assertiveness. People are aggressive, or conversely, relaxed.

I thus made up a 2x2 people matrix, with four elements. The four types of people are:

1. Aggressive and competent, also referred to as the Big Gun.

2. Aggressive but incompetent, otherwise known as the

Pretender and Phony.

3. Competent but relaxed, also known as the Has Been.
4. Incompetent and relaxed, also known as the Bumbling or Hapless Jerk.

A well-kept secret is that a goal in life is to become a Has Been. The Has Been is relaxed, comfortable, and at ease with life. The Has Been was previously a Big Gun, then opted to get out of the battle. Has Beens are indeed useful people. When you need a letter of recommendation, ask a Has Been. They write glowing letters. The Phony, in contrast, builds himself up by belittling those around him and especially under him.

Each of these four types of people has unique traits. The actions of each can be predicted. The problem is that #1 and #2 tend to appear indistinguishable. Moreover, #2 is the danger. The Pretender acts as a human roadblock. He or she will take credit for the work of others, but will pass the blame for failures onto others.

In the workplace, it is imperative that you be able to distinguish the #2 from the #1. One easy test for spotting a Phony, the #2, is simple. The Phony will never speak to you in language that you understand. They will deliberately speak above your head and use jargon you aren't familiar with. If a Phony is at an art exhibit, he will describe the artwork using musical terms, going on about the rhythm, the treble, the off-tones, and such. Conversely, when the Phony goes to a music performance, he will discuss the music using artistic language, using words like perspective, brush stroke, and tints. Phonies are easy to spot and unmask as long as you have prepared subroutines.

As I sit here typing, my mind is awash with subroutine topics. Consider that your child is at risk when getting off the school bus. The neighbor's vicious boxer dog—which is never on a leash—has shown aggressive and killer instincts. It even killed your son's six pet rabbits. You fear for the safety and even the life of your child. In my situation, we lived out in the country. As much as I tried, I wasn't always able to be there to greet my son. The walk from the bus drop-off to the house was 800 feet. Tim was then age eight. I instructed him to not run if attacked, but what kid really grasps that reality? I had a problem. My subroutine solved the problem.

I have literally thousands of prepared subroutines for dealing with all sorts of daily problems and situations. Although of interest, the fuller discussion and detailing of my subroutine library will have to be set aside for the time being.

Being a Mechanical Engineer

MY REFLECTIONS about choosing mechanical engineering as a career are many. I authored a full volume, *Circling the Drain: Humorous Musings on Becoming a Mechanical Engineer.* What follows is but a quick glimpse at some of the ways mechanical engineers are negatively treated and discounted by society.

Let us pretend that the world is facing some complex and overwhelming problem. To illustrate the point, I will jump into the question of *climate change*, or possibly some variation such as *global man-made warming.* Let us also suppose that somebody, notably a mechanical engineer, has analyzed the problem and has the answer. I assert that the world is in no way interested in what the mechanical engineer has to say.

By and large, mechanical engineers end up becoming losers. Once a mechanical engineer does something, he or she ceases to be needed. Moreover, the greater society seldom remembers the mechanical engineer's contributions.

Over the past century, mechanical engineers have invented and perfected three things, all related to the automobile:

- The electric starter
- Power assists like power steering and power brakes
- The automatic transmission

The driving public now has free access to automobiles and

mobility. A century ago, when cars had to be hand-cranked to start, driving was restricted to those strong enough to crank the engine. Steering required beefsteak. Driving was also limited to those with mechanical skills.

Today, virtually anybody can operate a car as long as they can reach the pedals. This gives people a feeling of empowerment. Jerks weave in and out of traffic lanes, with scant consideration for others. Mechanical engineers are not thanked or even remembered. There is something to be said about the good old days. Now, vast numbers think they are masters of their destinies—able to crank and start an engine, and leap tall buildings in a single bound.

Lemmings

AT THE BEGINNING of this *Dumb Dickie* book, I listed some dumb things I was told as a kid. I was told that lemmings rush to the sea, diving off cliffs and committing suicide. The myth still survives.

Lemmings are small rodents that live in Arctic and permafrost regions. Lemmings do exhibit unusual population cyclical swings. Approximately every fourth year or so when the thaw melts, in the year of the "high," referring to high population, lemmings are plentiful. The population cyclical swings are immense. Swings as high as 100 to 1, and even 1,000 to 1, can occur.

People who study lemmings are called lemmingologists. The crowning achievement in lemmingologist circles is to be correct in predicting the year of the high. Predictions are difficult, as at times it isn't the fourth year. It can be the third, the fourth, or the fifth.

Theories to explain what is causing the population cycles abound. One theory is that they are controlled by sunspots. Another theory is that the swings are a result of the classic predator-prey dynamics. Both of these theories are wrong. The proof is simple.

In Northern Canada, there is a large lake known as Great

Slave Lake. On that lake there are islands. One large island, called Eight-Mile Island, has its own lemming population.

The dynamics of the lemming population cycles on Eight-Mile Island are not synchronous with the population cyclical swings on the surrounding mainland. This immediately rules out sunspots. The Eight-Mile Island population cycles also rule out predator-prey dynamics. There are three major predators of lemmings, two of which are winged. The snowy owl is the dominant predator. Snowy owls can fly. The predator-prey hypothesis is thus refuted, as the owls can easily fly between the island and the mainland.

Dumb Dickie has stuck his nose out on other profound mysteries, so it is time to venture into the question behind lemming population cycles.

Lemmings experience population cycles because lemmings don't wear hats. I will explain.

In Austria, because of the mountainous terrain, many people inadvertently ended up marrying people they were related to, such as first and second cousins. The Austrian people solved this problem by wearing hats of different colors. Each family had a unique color of hat, and the rule was to only date and marry somebody wearing a different color of hat. The inbreeding problem was solved.

Lemmings don't wear hats. Under the snow as the year of the high approaches, much inbreeding takes place. The lemming populations experience dramatic cyclical swings because of this inbreeding; one aspect of the inbreeding is that it leads to a skewed sex ratio with more females than males, which in turn can lead to overpopulation in a shorter period of time. When the lemming population jumps, such as a thousand-fold, the summer thaw causes many of them to drown. The lemmings aren't committing suicide. They just aren't good long-distance swimmers and there are just too many of them. They have few places to go to escape the thaw waters. It's dark all winter, but the short summer brings a quick surface thaw. The lemmings tend to drown as their burrows fill with melted snow and ice water. The water can't drain away as the region is on top of permafrost.

The Philosophy of Dumbness

As I reflect back, dumbness happens because the person is operating under a set of logic rules that seem perfectly rational at the time, but in fact are flawed. A friend and former colleague in control systems, Dr. William B. Rouse, summed up life this way, "Every person is and acts as an optimal controller." In order to appreciate the application to humans, it is first helpful to comment on optimal control.

There are two basic ingredients to optimal control. First there is a definition as to what is best—thus optimal. Second, there is the control strategy: the action that is put into place for achieving that best or optimal outcome. The mathematical foundation of optimal control theory thus starts with the premise that somebody in advance has defined what is optimal. It could be as simple as amassing money. It could be golfing under a certain handicap. It could be getting the most life out of a car. It could be winning a race like the Indy 500. It could be slicing a tomato so thin that one tomato lasts until the next shopping trip. It could be just being lazy and seeking to avoid work. It could be the goal of winning the lottery. It could be refusing to ever buy a lottery ticket.

What is best depends upon the definition of best. That varies according to each person and his or her preferences. In order to give this a fancy name, mathematicians and systems specialists call the objective the *Index of Performance*, or commonly the *IP*. Once the IP is established, an optimal controller creates the decision or action that best drives one towards the IP. It is this action that causes the outcome to move in the direction of being optimal. The strategy is to best cause the system's outcome to be maximized, whereby the maximization of the IP is achieved.

Consider a boater, such as my father, who ends up in a sinking boat while midstream. He was duck hunting on the Housatonic River near his home in Stratford, Connecticut when his duck boat sank. Pop had to swim to shore. His IP or Index of Performance was to get to shore. Swimming in a river towards shore requires that a decision be made. What direction will get Pop to shore the quickest? Mathematicians have examined this as an optimization problem. The swimmer has to continually make decisions on which direction will get one to shore the quickest. The problem becomes more complex when currents are present. Humans typically do not swim taking the best route. In contrast, dogs have an uncanny ability to swim optimally. Mathematicians search for the best path to shore as dog curves.

My point is that determining an optimal way to achieve a goal is often not obvious. Mathematical techniques can be employed. These fall under the general classification of optimization, also called *variational calculus*. Optimal control is a rich topic. Whether a human's actions in pursuit of happiness are optimal or not, the desire to achieve maximum happiness is universal.

In my father's case, when his duck boat sank, his happiness goal included saving his possessions in addition to himself. Pop was a strong swimmer. He swam to shore while doing two other things. He swam with one arm up and out of the water—holding his precious shotgun above water. He also pushed his duck decoys along ahead of him to save them. All humans attempt to act as optimal controllers. Some humans do it better than others.

Nonetheless, all strive to maximize happiness.

An underlying trait of humans is the pursuit of happiness. Whatever we do, we do it because we perceive that it will increase our happiness. What might be later viewed as being a dumb thing to do was actually a deliberate and calculated action on the part of the person. The action was taken at the time based on the premise that happiness would result, or at least be increased.

I jumped out of a tree because doing so made me happy at the time of the jump. The hurt came later, actually very soon after, but at the precise moment of the jump I was doing something I thought would make me happier and thereby increase my overall happiness.

I must confess that I have never purchased a lottery ticket in my lifetime, nor am I likely to ever do so. People who purchase lottery tickets have a defined IP. Their objective is to take a position that will maximize the best of all possible outcomes. The state lottery programs have a different IP, that being to maximize their income, hence profit. The state lottery makes a profit because the law of large numbers works to their benefit. If any state government lost money by operating the lottery, the lottery sales would end. In my case, I win the lottery every time by not playing it. If I have a dollar in my pocket and don't buy the lottery ticket, then I still have my dollar. Conversely, the person who invests in the lottery ticket gains in happiness as they await the drawing. They dream that their ship will finally come in. Some rationalize it by thinking that it will be his or her turn, as if winning the lottery is something that is dispensed according to turns. The buyers of lottery tickets commonly achieve a sense of happiness that is short-lived. In their minds, they might just possibly win.

I strongly believe in the value of accomplishing small deeds and gains daily. Some have a notion that their fortune is pinned on their ship sailing in, all in one sudden huge lump. Perhaps their life's ambition is to win the Power Ball or the Irish Sweepstakes. My approach is to keep my efforts directed toward gaining a little each and almost every day. My ship does come in, but it comes in gradually, though steadily.

One strong motivation in writing about my dumb episodes is to hopefully cause future readers to become more worldly and wiser. As we age and gain experience, we hopefully improve on how we make our decisions, the decisions that are inherently based on a desire to increase happiness. I want my grandchildren to see life from a broader view. I want them to know that whatever problems might face them, they have the inner strength and decision-making ability to prevail and even prosper. I want my readers and kin to be as happy and successful in life as possible.

Please also recall that one earlier expressed purpose for telling the Dumb Dickie stories was to establish a central point: I am not holding myself out as perfect and being above making mistakes. I have made many other mistakes in my life. The Dumb Dickie episodes shared in this collection were selected mostly because of the inherent humor, the value of the lessons learned, and the relative ease in describing each dumb mistake.

Predestination vs. Freewill

BECAUSE WE HAVE TOUCHED ON certain theological and spiritual topics, I feel it appropriate to address yet one additional theological subject. I have come to believe in predestination. Being known at this point as Dumb Dickie, I will be dumb enough to wrestle with that beastly topic.

My son, Timothy, has a doctorate from the University of Minnesota. He works in high energy particle physics. Tim deals with abstract things that the human eye can't see or even visualize. I don't know all the terminology, but he speaks of things like quarks, neurons, pizo-whatevers, and such. He rattles off things about basic particles that have half-lives so small that I am lost. Tim Klein can't see what he deals with, and frankly doesn't even try. Tim's world is a world of relationships expressed by equations and probabilities. His world is very real. Tim works for a think-tank that resorts to high energy theory to strengthen our national defenses. Tim's work is so secret that if he ever told me what he does, he would have to kill me or banish me to the far side of Mars or possibly some distant quark.

Mathematicians deal with abstract things that can't be visualized by humans. To a mathematician, space isn't our kind of space but rather a set of rules, sometimes referred to as topology. Space has properties, one being distance. Distance can be as the crow flies or it can be how far we have to walk if we must stay on sidewalks. Distance has no meaning until and unless distance is first defined. Mathematicians first define distances and even space.

In the Bible, God defines, or at least gives us hints, that both Heaven and Earth have vastly different rules and behavioral properties. Sadly, but also joyously, in Heaven our human bodies are no longer required. I know that Heaven will be joyous beyond my ability to measure. I love the sight and company of beautiful women, but that pleasure will be replaced by something much more grand and spectacular.

Imagine a slowly moving river or stream. A rock or obstruction like a fallen tree can cause a little cascade or waterfall. The water flowing in that waterfall has properties similar to time. If a finger is inserted into the waterfall, the flow is altered downstream.

Freewill assumes and requires the presence of time. A property of time and freewill is that if one inserts a finger, the upstream can't be altered. Freewill assumes that our actions can only alter the future and not the past.

The problem gets stickier. If one inserts a finger into a waterfall as described, the falling water rejoins the slower river. The slower river will send information of its presence back up the river, even upstream of the little waterfall.

Our Earthly existence is analogous to the waterfall. That waterfall is trapped in a much larger river, a river I will refer to as Heaven.

Predestination and freewill can co-exist and be in harmony. The fact that we can't see beyond our waterfall, or time-space bubble, does not mean that nothing exists beyond what we can see. God has made wonderful provisions for us, available to all who believe in Him.

As an engineer and mathematician, but mostly mathematician, I cannot help but note the mathematical properties of Heaven. Although I can't see Heaven, I can infer its character and properties.

When I think of Heaven, I only have to imagine a soap bubble. Another name is a membrane, a membrane that is stretched. Kids can make soap membranes by dipping a bent hoop into a soapy solution. I envision Heaven as God reaching out His arms, joining them at the fingertips to create the hoop. The membrane or soap bubble formed within God's arms is Heaven. Moreover, when we become a part of Heaven, God is embracing all believers to be part of the whole.

Soap bubbles have amazing properties. The surface is perfectly smooth, also known as an analytical function. There are no discontinuities. For those with a background in mathematics, the soap bubble's surface or contour is so smooth that it has an infinite number of continuous derivatives. Every piece of a soap bubble, no matter how small or insignificant, has complete and perfect knowledge of the entire soap bubble's shape or configuration.

There are no secrets in Heaven and no secrets in soap bubbles. Every speck of a soap bubble is vital for the existence of the whole. Soap bubbles are indeed grandiose and magnificent. Similarly, so is Heaven. Only those forgiven of their sins by the blood of Christ are allowed to enter Heaven and be a part of His Kingdom. No discontinuity or sin, no matter how tiny, can be allowed. The slightest of pin pricks will cause a membrane to fail. Sin is not allowed in Heaven.

Because I view the world through a prism of mathematics, it is mathematical reasoning that allows me to resolve, in my mind at least and to my satisfaction, the long-standing and perplexing *predestination versus freewill* seeming paradox. I will again state my world view: predestination and freewill are not inherently incompatible. The entire argument boils down to the fact that God stands outside of time. God is not trapped in the flow of time. We as humans are trapped like particles flowing along in a river called time. God is not so constrained.

Yet More on Theology

THE ABOVE DISCUSSION of Dumb Dickie stories implies some role of what I'll call the supernatural and inherently my theology. A natural tendency for many secular persons is to discount any such suggestions, in particular regarding the realm of the supernatural. For me, I don't have that luxury.

Certain events have occurred in my lifetime. It would be delusionary for me to deny they ever happened. These events have forced me to deal with reality. I can't just brush my history aside by saying it never happened. As a man of science and mathematics, I am able to recognize when events unfolded in a pattern in stark conflict with what can be described as the laws of probability or random chance.

I am fully aware, for example, that the Murphy story is particularly gruesome in its detail. If I would have left out the gruesome detail, the story would have far less impact. Another strange observation is that at times in my life events have defied what I will call causality. The telling of that aspect will have to be set aside for the present.

In my own case, I have kept consistent journals of my life and thoughts for the better part of the last one-third of a century. Starting in 1983, I have kept meticulous journal notes. Each journal is 300 pages in length. I am presently finishing up my

22nd such journal. This amounts to approximately 6,600 pages of journal notes. Rest assured, if some skeptic or doubter would ever wish to challenge me on my facts and assertions, I have the ability to provide an immense amount of detail supporting my claims. In those journal entries I have made numerous annotations concerning the circumstances of an array of, let's say, unusual happenings. At present, I will defer delving any deeper.

At this point I will merely close and wish a blessed life and happiness to each and every one of my readers.

IN CLOSING

THE LIFE AND TIMES of Dumb Dickie has been a lengthy and yet exciting journey. In the story, on December 24, 1963 I threw a ham through a car's windshield. My new bride Marjorie wasn't prepared for such a violent act emanating from her docile, friendly, and polite husband. In hindsight, I see that Marjorie was motivated to marry me as I offered adventure and travel. Her other suitors were typically focused on raising hogs on an Iowa farm, having kids, and remaining on the farm, with her becoming a dutiful housewife. Well, it is fair to say that Marjorie never lacked for adventure and travel in our life together.

As I look back at my life, there is little or actually nothing I would change. I've had a wonderful life. I also hope that I have somehow made a difference in the world—to make the world a better place. Many or even most of my accomplishments were fleeting and hard for an outside observer to see.

One accomplishment in my life is the adapted bike program, a program that permits children with disabilities to discover the joy that comes with riding a two-wheeler. Before I entered into that quest, the world accepted the fact that children with disabilities were incapable of mastering bike riding. I am not talking about training wheels, four-wheeled contraptions, and such, but ordinary conventional two-wheelers. As of 2019, approximately 30,000 children with varied disabilities have leaped into a new world—a world of bike riding and feeling the wind in their faces.

Parents are grateful, almost to the point of tears of joy. It isn't easy being Dumb Dickie. When I attend bike camps, I am at times attacked. Sobbing women rush up to me, crushing me with hugs. Their child can now ride a two-wheeler. In some cases, the parents had tried for as long as ten years and had failed. In the adapted bike program, children commonly master bike riding within the camps' five-day format.

Hemingway remarked that a man should do four things in his lifetime:

- Plant a tree
- Write a book
- Father a son
- Fight a bull

I've done all four, provided you grant me the right to call a 4,000-pound car accelerated directly at me as equivalent to a bull charging at me.

Yes, I have enjoyed a wonderful life. I also thank and acknowledge God and God's helper Herman, my guardian angel.

BONUS MATERIAL

Revisiting Broken Stud Removal Options

THIS MATERIAL is technical in nature. It has little to do with how to do dumb things. In contrast, it explains how to successfully remove a broken stud, such as in an engine block.

Now as I write this story in 2019, some 60 years after the fact, my appreciation for and grasp of machinist skills have grown by leaps and bounds. At this point I am digressing so as to educate my younger generation of readers. Please bear with me. Assume that a similar situation would pop up today. Also assume that the broken stud was deeply rusted and stuck in place. Of course in this situation, if possible, I would take the entire car with its engine to a qualified machinist. Note that I use the word machinist, as opposed to mechanic. Absent that, such as if I was on the far side of Timbuktu, if I attempted the job myself here is how I would proceed. This task is serious business. One usually can't afford mistakes. Once the job starts, there is seldom a second chance. In my mind, only one safe and fail-proof option exists, that being to drill out the broken stud and to then restore the original threads in the cast iron engine block. With this in mind, my approach would be the following:

1. I would first grind the face of the broken stud flat, especially at its center. A small powered die grinder would do this easily. If even a slight protrusion existed, an

angle grinder would suffice. Grinding will make it easier for the drill to stay on center and not wander about.

2. I would determine the inside diameter of the threads in the block. That determination is fairly easy as all studs of SAE (English) design have standardized thread specifications. Knowing the stud diameter normally would tell me the internal ID of the threads in the block. This can be determined by referring to a machinist's handbook given the stud's diameter. One could alternatively contact a dealership and get the specification from their service department. An Internet or chat-board search would also provide the desired diameter.

3. The next surprise move would be to reinstall the head that had been previously removed from the engine. There is no need for a head gasket. The purpose for reinstalling the head is only to temporarily allow the head itself to serve as a bushing guide for drilling. The primary objective is clear: to drill directly in line with the center of the broken stud. So long as the head is positioned on the other remaining intact studs, it would suffice to secure the head in place with just a few lightly tightened nuts.

4. Because the hole diameter in the head is too large, I would find or have a machinist make a suitable bushing or sleeve. If I lacked such a bushing, these can be ordered from standard industrial supply houses, such as Granger Industrial Supply or Enco Industrial Supply. It is only important to select a bushing with a proper outside diameter (OD) so that the bushing will drop nicely but also snugly into the head. The inside diameter of the bushing can vary within limits, as the choice of drill bit diameter isn't critical at this point. The immediate objective is to drill a pilot hole directly on center in the broken stud. Moreover, the skilled machinist would

possibly start the hole by first using a self-centering drill.

Shown above is a set of self-centering drill bits. They are used, often in a milling machine, to start a hole precisely on center. These drill bits are designed specifically for the purpose of starting the hole. Once the hole has been suitably started, then the machinist can switch over to a standard drill bit. In a perfect world, I would select my bushing to permit the use of a self-centering drill. Again, getting the drill started in the center is critical. After the hole had been started, I would then select a drill bit diameter that matched the OD of the self-centering drill. The objective is to drill a pilot hole down all the way through the broken stud. With the head in place and by using a bushing to keep the drill bit in proper alignment, the hole in the broken stud will be on center.

5. That broken stud piece is typically about an inch deep. Once the drill penetrates the depth of the broken stud piece, one hits a void or air pocket. When the drill bit breaks through, the drill will quickly bottom out. The drill is retracted from the hole at this point. No harm occurs to the block itself even though the drill bit has momentarily bottomed out.

6. Now the broken stud has been drilled through and directly on center. The head can now be removed as it

has served its purpose. Assuming that the pilot hole was undersize, say ¼ or 5/16 inch in diameter, it is then a straightforward matter to drill out the broken stud to the diameter of the ID of the threads, or just slightly under. As a perfectionist, I would select the drill bit diameter to be about 0.010" or possibly 0.020" less in diameter than the ID of the threads in the cast iron block. The drilling in this operation will enlarge the hole's diameter. Moreover, the larger drill will closely follow the pilot hole.

7. The task has now been reduced to one of removing the thin-walled shell of the former stud. The objective is to remove the thin shell and yet not damage or compromise the threads in the cast iron block. By using some penetrating oil or rust dissolver, the remaining thread material from the broken stud can often be loosened up. After allowing adequate time for the penetrating oil to do its job, I would then attempt to remove the remaining thread material. My first approach would be to use a small steel chisel or even a sharp punch or awl. This pointed tool can be lightly tapped with a hammer. My objective is to cause the thin remaining shell of the broken stud with its threads to collapse inward. If I am able to start a collapse, then the matter of additional collapsing becomes simple. At times, use of needle-nose pliers will permit the deformed and collapsed shell to be twisted out and thereby removed. A second approach would be to use an acetylene torch to heat up the thin shell. It is amazing how much a torch can prevail over rusted and stuck parts. The shell is quite thin at this point. Having little mass, it will heat up quickly. Moreover, the rust between the shell and the cast iron threads in the block will cease to be an issue. Following application of heat, one should be able to dislodge and collapse the shell of the drilled out stud.

8. An alternative to Step #7 is to drill the broken stud out to its inside thread diameter. This will leave a series of spiral-shaped strips still embedded in the threads in the block. The objective now is to somehow dislodge the spiral portions of the thread material. It isn't necessary to get all of the thread material out, but only some near the face of the block. The goal is to be able to get a tap started so that the tap can and will follow the original threads. At that point one could use a standard thread tap to go in and clean out the threads. Because threads already exist in the cast iron engine block, the tap will usually follow the existing threads. Nonetheless, exacting care should be used. As in all tapping operations, and this one in particular, it is important to periodically clear the tap. After several turns or whenever the tap feels tight, one backs off by reversing direction. At times it is helpful to remove the tap so as to clean out the flutes. Once one is assured that the tap is following the old threads, cleaning the threads with a tap set is straightforward. Of course, when using any tap, one should apply liberal amounts of cutting oil. The task using taps boils down to cleaning out threads in the stud hole. Because it is a blind hole, one would normally use three different taps in succession. These are the tapered tap, then a half-tapered tap, and finally what is called a bottoming tap. Once the threads are cleared, compressed air can be used to clear the stud hole of any remaining chips and debris.

9. Because I strive for completeness, the reader attempting this procedure should be aware that studs can have two different thread standards. The exposed or top threads are typically coarse (national coarse). The threads inside the block are in some cases fine threads, known as NF (national fine). Knowing the difference in advance is crucial. In the above discussion of thread standards, I have

assumed that the engine conforms to SAE (English) thread standards.

At this point it is straightforward to install a new replacement stud.

It would take a skilled machinist about 30 minutes to perform all of these steps. Most good machinists would have the necessary drill bits and even the bushing on hand. Absent any needed tools or the bushing, overnight delivery would remedy the problem.

Heat helps when dealing with anything rusted and tight, especially heat from an acetylene torch. As a cautionary note, the use of an acetylene torch in many applications requires considerable skill. The amateur is advised to use extreme caution.

Another option available to a machinist is to first weld a washer in place on the exposed flat of the broken stud. The preferred welder is referred to as the TIG welder. Next, a nut is welded onto the washer and stud. The welding has the additional benefit of heating the broken stud's remains thus dislodging the rust. Then, a wrench or socket set can be applied to turn the broken stud out.

In extreme cases, the skilled machinist can use a thing called a Helicoil®, which effectively creates new threads when the urgency requires. This option assumes that the broken off stud or bolt has been drilled out using a somewhat larger drill size.

The above cutaway image from the Internet shows a Helicoil® in place in a casting. The idea is to tap threads of a larger diameter in the casting and then insert a spiral coil that will restore the threads to the original specification. This procedure can also be employed should the original hole become stripped out or too large in diameter.

As an advisory note, I should stress that I seldom purchase drill bits from hardware and home improvement stores. They sell notoriously cheap drill bits. Instead, I purchase only top-of-the-line drill bits from vendors that specialize in tools for the professional. Cheap drill bits are soft and soon lose their sharpness. The abrasion without good chip removal creates heat, which accelerates the failure of the drill bit.

Another observation is that the skilled machinist would have recognized the problem of a stuck or rusted nut on an engine or project in the first place. Some common options to prevent a stud from shearing off begin with approaching the nut removal process differently. One option is to first apply penetrating oil to dissolve the rust. Dissolving embedded rust takes time, so don't get in a hurry. A second option would be to apply heat to the nut with an acetylene torch prior to attempting to loosen the nut(s). The proper temperature is a dull cherry red. Once the nut is dull cherry red, the removal of the nut becomes incredibly trivial. Also, as the hot nut begins to cool, penetrating oil will work to dissolve rust. Yes, the penetrating oil will sizzle a little, but keep pouring it on. A third option for the machinist is to use a steel chisel and hammer to split the nut and break it free. This option would be a consideration especially if the use of a torch would be too risky such as due to adjacent fuel lines. A fourth option would be to use an angle grinder or die grinder to cut a slice in the nut. If the cut isn't complete, a steel chisel and machinist's hammer can often finish the job by splitting the nut loose. In any of these four options, the machinist will follow up the nut removal by running a die over the threads of the stud, thus chasing the threads.

Of all the options above, the one most frequently used and

preferred is the use of a torch. Note that muffler and exhaust shops routinely use torches to remove old nuts and exhaust system hangers. The cost of the new nuts and hangers is trivial, as what is most costly in any professional shop is time. Yet another advantage of using a torch is that one size fits all. The torch, quite frankly, doesn't need to know the exact diameter of the nut size. Also, the torch doesn't even care if the nut is SAE (English) or SI (metric). By using a torch on stud nuts, the studs are never damaged because the heat doesn't rise too much in the stud. Only the nut being heated becomes a dull cherry red.

I recently spoke with my machinist, Steve Smith, regarding how he would approach the broken stud problem. Steve agreed that the use of the removed head as a bushing guide was an excellent way to go. Steve also commented about how to properly use an Easyout®. In that case Steve would first drill a proper hole in the broken stud, suitable for using an Easyout®. He would then apply heat to the broken stud. As the broken stud was cooling, he would apply generous amounts of penetrating oil. Lastly, given Steve's ability as a master machinist, he would attempt the extraction. The trick is in not overdoing the twisting moment because if the Easyout® breaks, the problem becomes vastly more complex.

As for me, if I never use an Easyout® again in my entire lifetime I won't be sad. I have become skilled and comfortable with drilling. The use of the head with a bushing as a drill guide will take most of the guesswork out.

"Too soon we get old and too late we get smart."

Prayers and Prayers Answered: My Testimony

I AM INCLUDING a letter I wrote several years ago. I trust that the letter and its contents are self-explanatory.

February 5, 2014

Greetings to my family—my children and grandchildren (and friends by extension),

This spring I have been taking a Bible-oriented course on Wednesday evenings at church. The subject matter is the Book of Acts, taught by Dr. Greg Perry of Covenant Theological Seminary in St. Louis. In the process, Dr. Perry has given the class a challenging "homework" assignment. I am to compose a letter of my personal testimony, addressed to some particular person or persons, regarding my journey of faith in coming to Christ. Each of us is the foremost expert (authority) on our personal life, and as such each of us doesn't have to resort to library research or Google internet sources. The purpose of this letter is to document my personal story. My personal story is unique to me, and upon reflection, it is something that is critical that I write. Here goes...

My personal walk with and final acceptance of Jesus Christ as my Lord and Savior is long and complex. Moreover, it spans many years. I will talk about three incidents, and all three relate to prayers (or requests) that I made in moments of intense stress, and how these prayers were answered. As the writer, it is my prerogative to put these in an order of my choosing, so I will start with the most recent and then work backwards in time.

PRAYER #3

During February 1983, it was my custom to telephone my mother, then living in Stratford, Connecticut. Pop (my father) lived there as well, but I say "mother" because Mother was the one who would answer the telephone. By then my father's mental and physical state had been in deterioration. The primary purpose of my call (from my home in Dewey, Illinois) was to check on the status of things. It was somewhat late in the evening. I would venture to say that it must have been about 11 p.m. Eastern Time. Mother answered the phone, and here is the gist of what she had to say about how things were going.

Because the house was a two-story, the bedrooms were upstairs, but each day they would spend the day on the first floor. Pop's ability to climb stairs was in serious doubt. I asked Mother how Pop was able to climb the stairs. She replied that she would get behind him and help lift him as he climbed the steps. Then she went on to say that yes, she had gotten Pop to the upper hallway and into his bedroom, but that he had fallen next to the bed and was unable to get up and that she lacked the strength to help lift him. I then asked if Mother had called for help, such as somebody to come and to get Pop into bed, or possibly see that he was removed from the house and taken elsewhere where care could be provided. What my mother said next floored me. Her decision had been to leave him lay, but that she did cover him with a blanket. I didn't ask if that included putting a pillow under his head. Please bear in mind that it was still February in Connecticut—and my father was unconscious or otherwise unresponsive on a cold floor.

When I challenged Mother as to why she was not doing more, she said the following: (1) He will be dead by morning; and (2) the idea of calling for an ambulance or other help was not going to happen because she feared that no good would come of it other than all her savings in life would be consumed. We chatted for a little more, and the phone call ended. At that point I held onto the phone trying to assimilate the enormity of what I had just heard. I knew that I was virtually powerless to do anything, except pray for my father. I was also under an obligation to honor my mother's decision, as she was no stranger to making hard decisions, especially when it concerned doctors whom she distrusted. I said a prayer to God wherein I asked for God's mercy on my father, and in particular that he should live the night and even live another ten years. At the time in February 1983, my father, Albert W. Klein, was then aged 72. He was born November 21, 1910.

Miraculously, my father lived that night, and his physical health gradually improved. He and Mother sold the house in Stratford a little over a year later. They moved in the summer of 1984 to the small town of Wessington Springs, South Dakota. Their new home was a ranch type, so it involved no climbing of steps. That town was selected as my Mother had numerous kin living there, including 17 first cousins at the time. By having nearby family, she had support and the ability to enjoy a social life. With Pop's dementia, the truth was that it mattered little where he was because his world had grown to be so small. The town was small (population about 1,500) and had nowhere for Pop to wander off into. In Connecticut, with about 50 cents in hand Pop could have gotten onto a public bus and become lost in the large city comprised of Bridgeport and the adjoining eastern end of Fairfield County.

Some years went by, and my father's physical health improved so much that a favorite pastime was playing golf, something beyond my wildest imaginations. Pop was eventually committed to a nursing home, actually one and then a second as his needs increased. Along the way he made a mistake—he took a slug at a doctor. Doctors don't like getting attacked, so Pop was both drugged and restrained. The restraints and not being able to walk caused muscle atrophy. Pop passed away in March of 1993—ten years and one month after my prayer that he live another ten years.

PRAYER #2

Marjorie and I had our first child in 1973, a daughter we named Victoria. Over the ensuing years, we then tried to have more children, but for a while either pregnancy didn't happen, or in two cases Marjorie experienced miscarriages. At the same time, in the 1970s I had invested in some Illinois farm land (80 acres in Homer in 1973). My initial investment leaped in value, to the point that I was able to borrow on the Homer farm and get enough cash to buy a small hotel in Naples, Florida. The purchase price was $525,000. The land values in Florida then leaped and the hotel was eventually sold for about $1.3M, unfortunately not for cash but by swapping assets. By the late 1970s, I had a net worth of about $2M—and yet no second child.

One night I said a quiet prayer to God that if He would bless Marjorie and me with a second child, I would gladly give up all the assets and wealth I had accumulated. Two things happened: (1) Marjorie conceived, and gave birth to Timothy in March of 1980, and (2) my economic fortunes went into a tailspin. The hotel had been exchanged for two farms in Iowa (over 500 acres combined), using what is called a Section 1031 tax-free exchange. I was invested in Iowa farmland, and then the bottom fell out. I went from having a $2M net worth (in 1979), to being about $800,000 in the arrears (in the 1984 era). I had debt obligations that I could not service. I was faced with bankruptcy, or stalling that off, somehow shaking off the creditors. I engaged an attorney who was able to negotiate the debt away because I deeded all three farm parcels back to the various creditors. I avoided bankruptcy, but my life's savings were wiped off the slate. But, I had the son I so dearly wanted and had prayed for. There is absolutely no question that God answered my prayer.

I also marvel at the ability for an investor to lose $2M and so quickly. I wasn't throwing dice or spinning a roulette wheel in Las Vegas. Instead, each financial move I made was done with the knowledge and blessings of my banker. I'll say it this way: I defy you to entirely wipe out an investment of $2M in such a short period with the restriction that you could only make investment moves that were approved in advance by your banker.

PRAYER #1

This prayer is by far the most complex, so please bear with me. Moreover, as an expediency towards brevity I will try to be as concise as possible.

I obtained my Ph.D. in 1968 and started teaching at the University of Illinois. After two years of living in Champaign, thus in the spring of 1970, Marjorie and I had accumulated some savings. My office mate, Richard L. Shell, was about to leave the University, so he and his wife invited Marjorie and me to their home for coffee, with the expressed purpose of selling us their home at 905 West Green Street, Champaign. For our first two years Marjorie and I had rented what I call a modest English apartment, meaning it was a basement apartment that one entered by going down ½ a flight of steps. We enjoyed our coffee that night. Dick Shell then wrote a number on a piece of paper to indicate his asking price. We had agreed there would be no haggling, but rather a simple yes or no. I was amazed that Dick wrote down a price of $34,100. Marjorie and I had previously decided we would go as high as $36,000. Remember that in 1970 one could buy a fairly nice house for the mid-thirties. We accepted the offer, and with little other than a handshake, the deal was done.

As Marjorie and I drove home, I remarked to her, "What we need now is a flood." My reasoning was that we had a lease agreement on our apartment that extended through the summer, but we were getting possession of the 905 West Green Street house in June. If a flood would come, then it would be an act of God that would allow us to breach the rental contract and move out without financial penalty. It was a Friday night.

The next night, Saturday night at about 3 a.m., a lady from the adjoining basement-level apartment knocked on our door. She had gotten up to go to the bathroom and had stepped in water. The water was rising and so she wanted to alert us. Obviously, it was raining heavily outside, but the water was entering because the sanitary sewer was backing up. Marjorie and I got up and started trying to lift our furniture and stuff so as to prevent water damage. I found some discarded concrete blocks behind the apartment building.

The next part of the story is complex, but I'll be brief. We had the previous year installed a new Kitchen Aid dishwasher, as the apartment lacked a dishwasher. I selected a regular model as opposed to a portable because I could save money. I had put it where the refrigerator had been, as there was a proper-sized break in the kitchen counter next to the sink. Being a permanent dishwasher, it needed to be wired with Romex (that is a trademark name) which I had fed inside a nearby 110-volt wall outlet. Said another way, the dishwasher was hard-wired behind a receptacle and didn't have a pull plug.

By then, the water was about three inches deep and as the song goes, "And rising." I was wearing an old pair of shoes to protect my feet, but I was constantly standing in water. I needed to undo or disconnect the Romex wire. I decided the best move would be to throw the breaker switch to "off" and just cut the exposed Romex with side-cutters. I went to our car, as that was where my tools were kept. I hunted for about 20 minutes, in the rain, and failed to find my side-cutters. Then it dawned on me.

Several days before when I was riding my bike to campus as a part of my then regular commute, I happened upon a pair of needle-nose electrical pliers on the pavement. I stopped, picked them up, and put them into my backpack. I had totally forgotten about them. Now, once I remembered them, I got them, threw the breaker off, and proceeded to cut the Romex—while standing inches deep in the basement flood and sewage water!!!

Well, I got the surprise of my life. The electrical line I was cutting into was hot. Sparks flew. I dropped the pliers. It was still dark out, so I hadn't killed all the power in the apartment but rather only the breaker for the dishwasher's circuit because I wanted some lights to continue to see with.

What saved my life was the fact that I used the "found" needle-nose pliers. By a freak quirk, they had insulated handles. My older regular lineman's pliers that I couldn't find lacked insulation protection. Without question, a person who cuts into a live 110-volt AC circuit using steel cutters while standing in water is dead—period. When I tell this story, I call it *The Story of*

3 ½ Miracles.

MIRACLE 1: I asked for a flood and I got my wish—and in just slightly over 24 hours.

MIRACLE 2: I was not able to find my old steel-handled side-cutters.

MIRACLE 3: God, not being bound by time, knew (in advance, and by several days) that I would need the "found" pliers that had the insulated grips.

THE HALF MIRACLE: God had to be busy at work so as to arrange the above three miracles in a specific order. The act of finding the insulated pliers would have been irrelevant if I had just retrieved and used my standard set of pliers without insulation. As an aside, I now strongly endorse using only pliers that have insulated grips.

I have told some people this story, most commonly students and co-workers, but over the years I have found that people listening are intrigued by my narratives, but instead of acclaiming Jesus Christ as their Lord and Savior, they instead ask me to tell them yet another story. On this point, yes, I have numerous additional stories to testify to (28 if my count is correct), but I have opted to only tell three in this letter. Jesus makes it clear that those who ask for yet another heavenly sign have already elected to ignore the many signs that God has already provided.

In my case as a strong and assertive young man, I didn't feel the need to have to depend on God. Instead, I would just do it myself and handle whatever problem I was facing. Yes, God now has my attention, but it took the proverbial 2x4 striking me on the head to get my attention. Moreover, it took more than one strike.

Love, peace and blessings to you all,
Richard E. Klein (Dad/Grandpa)
r-klein@illinois.edu

Ingredients for a Marriage

MARJORIE AND I have now passed our 55th anniversary mark. We have been asked at times what has worked to keep us together and seemingly happy. I can point to six ingredients. The first two were given to us by Dr. Donald Blackstone, the Presbyterian minister who married us in 1963. The third ingredient was providence, or just something about our inner beings. The fourth, fifth, and sixth we figured out along the way.

1. Get a joint checking account. All money and worldly possessions belong to both of us, not just one of us.

2. Be supportive of each other. It is easy to criticize the other guy. Look for the positive. Support each other.

3. Neither of us ever smoked. In the era when we were dating, smoking was incredibly common. Our parents and some siblings smoked. I will exaggerate a little, but it would be fair to say that nine out of ten college-aged people smoked. The chances of two non-smokers becoming engaged would be the product of 0.1 squared. Yes, Marjorie and I are one in a hundred. I will add that neither of us has the slightest desire to get a tattoo. If I ever did, I would have to go to great lengthhs to sea that my tato was spelled correctly. My mudder was abhoared

with my mispellings.

4. We developed a rule about nagging. Something could be said three times. Whatever the remark, it could be stated three times with no objection, opposition, or counter claim. When it went beyond three, the other person could say, "You're nagging." If saying it three times doesn't work, the fourth, fifth, or even sixth won't work either.

5. The fifth marital tranquility ingredient was the IFR (Instrument Flight Rules) read back. This phrase is used between air traffic control and pilots. An IFR clearance is not considered as delivered until and unless the pilot reads back the clearance. Marjorie and I used this practice in our marital communications. For example, upon departing in the morning for our respective jobs, each would read back his/her to-do list such as for errands after work. A critical component was always who was to pick up our children at the sitter's house. The practice of the read back avoided mix-ups and miscommunications.

6. The sixth ingredient stemmed from an inside joke that came from Robert, Marjorie's brother. We borrowed the joke. A bunch of guys were in a cabin somewhere. The deal was that if anybody complained about the food, that person became the new cook. One morning, the menu called for biscuits and gravy. Sausage was ground up to add to the gravy. The cook added some cayenne pepper to spice up the gravy. The biscuits and gravy were served. One guy shouted out, "Wow, this is sure spicy… but it's just the way I like it." Unknown to the cook, the ground sausage was already spiced. The cayenne pepper wasn't needed.

A common remark or reply in our relationship is, "It's just the way I like it." You can never change the other person, so it is destructive to try.

ACKNOWLEDGEMENTS

We all make mistakes and do dumb things. It's important that we recognize our mistakes and try to learn from them. The objective is to not repeat our mistakes. We can learn things on our own. We should also seek the advice of mentors. I am grateful for guidance, companionship, and good role modeling by others. As Newton remarked, we stand on the shoulders of giants, giants who have gone before us and who have extended a hand and generously shared their wisdom.

Many wise and caring people have aided me. I wish to acknowledge Arthur Keefe my Scoutmaster, Mary Olha my eighth-grade science teacher, Frank Lesneski Sr. who counseled me in street confrontation defensive skills, Dr. Donald Olson at Pennsylvania State University, Dr. Robert H. Kohr at Purdue University, Dr. Raymond Eugene "Gene" Goodson my doctoral advisor at Purdue University, Dr. Branny von Turkovich at the University of Illinois, Dr. Helmet L. Korst my first Department Head at the University of Illinois, and Dr. Rudolf E. Kalman who boosted the field of control systems in ways hard to measure. I had the privilege to associate personally with all except for Rudy Kalman. I did have the pleasure of meeting Kalman once at a conference and shaking hands with him. A second giant in my travels was Dr. James A. Yorke of the University of Maryland. I had interactions with Yorke prior to his achieving fame as the driving force that brought modern chaos theory into view.

I wish to thank the numerous students at the University of Illinois. I was the professor teaching but I learned more from my students than I could have ever taught them.

Thanks also to my parents for good genes.

ABOUT THE AUTHOR

Richard E. Klein, by his own admission, is an incurable romantic and altruist. His writings and musings are filled with hope and bright horizons despite having lived through World War II and the Korean War as a child, both of which deeply impacted his worldview. Through his books, he aims to point the way towards a better internal mindset and a better world.

Richard earned his Ph.D. in engineering from Purdue University in 1969 and taught systems theory for three decades at the University of Illinois in Urbana-Champaign before retiring in 1998. He holds a particular interest in bicycle stability and control, and has devoted much of his time and energy to the development of an international program for teaching children with disabilities to master bike riding. Visit iCanBike.org and RainbowTrainers.com for more specifics.

Richard and his wife of more than 55 years, Marjorie Maxwell Klein, reside in the St. Louis area. They have two children and six grandchildren. Richard writes for them and for generations to come.

We're All Set, *The Deadly Gamble*, and *Kisses When I Get Home* are some of Richard's books currently available, and he has others in various stages of writing and publication.

10786948R10185

Made in the USA
Monee, IL
02 September 2019